DARK TRUTHS

Modern Theories of Serial Murder

**Dr Christopher J Kurtz
and Robert D Hunter**

Other books by Christopher J Kurtz

Demons and Madmen

First published in Great Britain in 2004 by
Virgin Books Ltd
Thames Wharf Studios
Rainville Road
London
W6 9HA

A catalogue record for this book is available from the British Library.

ISBN 0 7535 0814 1

Typeset by TW Typesetting, Plymouth, Devon
Printed and bound in Great Britain by
Mackays of Chatham PLC

CONTENTS

INTRODUCTION

What drives a man to kill a person, and another, and then another, until he can no longer stop? Urges that possess a man to commit serial murder are no easier to understand than any other addictive compulsion. Irrational behaviour cannot be defined by rational thought. One can apply logic to a study of the motivations that drive maladaptive behaviour, but the investigator must suspend his or her dependence on rational cognition. It is a maddening exercise to attempt to make sense of something that defies typical explanation or simple categorisation. And yet it is necessary to attempt the nearly impossible, if we are ever to understand the serial killer and his motivations. Every little bit counts in the development of proactive strategies for early identification. Each piece holds implications for intervention and treatment.

Although this book applies a logical process to the study of serial killers, it does not define a universal set of principles. There are two reasons for this. Firstly, it is a subject that is too complex for any single school of thought to claim authority. Secondly, such a universal set would not take into account individual differences within a given subset of serial killers. In order to gain a more thorough understanding of serial murder, cross-disciplinary approaches are necessary. In an age of advanced specialisation, we have taken the disciplines of science, sociology and psychology to new depths of understanding. But, in the process, we have alienated the disciplines from one another. Specialisation is a pioneering process that cuts a narrow path, and improved communication between disciplines is a necessary step in developing a comprehensive model. Since there is no single causative factor to which the crime of serial murder can be attributed, experts in all fields need to throw their informed hat into the discussion to produce a meaningful and insightful dialogue into an enduringly complex crime.

If one could overcome the obstacles in developing an integrated model, it would be unlikely to take into account the diverse differences between serial killers. Each one has his own distinct signature and ritual. For this reason, the book examines five separate theories of serial murder. Each theory is followed by case studies of specific killers who match the criteria. The theories are derived from the authors' personal correspondence with these killers. In some cases, original observations are supplemented with adaptations of existing theories.

The theories outlined in this book have similarities, as well as differences. The challenge is not so much in identifying the similarities as it is in integrating the differences. Such an approach is essential in developing a comprehensive model of serial murder. It is the only way we can properly study the seemingly elusive beast that the serial killer has become over the past three hundred years.

1. A GENERAL DISTINCTION

The five theories of serial murder outlined in this book are interrelated. A common feature of each theory is the indication of low self-esteem. If regarded as a stimulus, this feature elicits a predictable response with a corresponding set of behaviours. But just as any two people react differently to a particular event, so do serial killers. Imagine how two separate individuals might respond to the death of a loved one. A predictable reaction might be to seek comfort from other loved ones who are also grieving the loss. But another reaction, just as predictable, could be to engage in isolation from others. The same is true of self-esteem. The expression of low self-esteem can be either overt or covert. It depends on a person's psychological disposition, which is generally considered to be a product of upbringing and individual experience. For some, its expression is obvious and the manifestations are well known to the person experiencing them; for others, it is less obvious and the manifestations are a product of the person's compensatory behaviours. In the latter case, the person often presents as overconfident with an inflated ego.

Killers of the first distinction portray an *overt* lack of self-esteem. Society has rejected these individuals; in some cases the individuals' perception of rejection has fuelled the reality of it. They want nothing more than to appreciate the acceptance of others. When this is not forthcoming, they resort to acquiring it by any means necessary. Since relationships have not proven stable and long lasting, they do not experience the usual barriers in rectifying the taking of a life. In other words, *they* are the victims. Often this is true. An investigation into the childhood of practically every serial killer reveals an appalling history of abuse. As their ill-fated attempts at building relationships continue to fail, they take excessive measures to meet their aims.

In the effort to experience a gratifying relationship, no matter how fleeting, they attempt to control the variables that impede the process of this desired outcome. Since others are unwilling to engage in a relationship with them, they believe that taking a victim is justifiable. Anticipating that they will always be rejected, they often abduct an unwilling partner to create a fantasy relationship. The relationship provides them with a transitory sense of security because the captor exercises complete control over the captive.

Obviously, this practice of acquiring submissive acceptance is short-lived. It necessitates repeating: thus, a series emerges. The process follows a logical pattern. The Offence Cycle Theory of murder defines a predictable sequence that repeats itself in the thoughts and actions of a serial killer. Murder becomes an addiction. The Fantasy Addiction Model also supports this theory, with particular attention given to the deviant fantasies that drive the act of murder. A third theory, the Medical Model of serial murder, examines how physiological impairments, whether the result of a traumatic injury or a specific condition, can sometimes lead to a propensity for murder.

Killers of the second distinction, that of the *covert* manifestation of low self-esteem, are far more difficult to identify. For one thing, their defence mechanisms are more sophisticated. They do not present themselves as lacking in self-esteem. If anything, they appear overly confident and sure of themselves. It must be understood, however, that this façade is in response to deep-seated feelings of rejection and inadequacy. They are so effective at compensating for these feelings that they generally lack awareness of their existence. Rather than acknowledge their poor ego strength, they develop the belief that they are superior to other human beings. Perhaps they feel that the world owes them something. Almost certainly, they feel that they are not getting the recognition they deserve. Often these killers are remarkably intelligent and articulate.

Because these killers possess intelligence and refined skills of manipulation, they are more difficult to apprehend than their less sophisticated counterparts. For one thing, they are more organised. Ted Bundy, for example, often lured victims by pretending to be helpless. He would fashion an artificial cast for his arm, then play on the sympathy of women who believed they were coming to his assistance when they observed him struggling to load boxes into the trunk of his Volkswagen. His disposal of the victims was also well planned. The bodies were hidden in such remote areas that many of them would probably never have been recovered had he not identified their locations to the police. Richard Trenton Chase, by contrast, made little effort to cover his tracks. Known as the Vampire of Sacramento, he eviscerated his victims and mutilated their internal organs, sometimes running them through an electric blender, in an effort to extract the blood for his consumption. He often smeared the blood on his face and neck and walked the streets in such a manner after leaving the scene of the crime, and wore the same blood-soaked clothes for days at a time. Clearly he fits the description of a disorganised killer.

The highly organised killer may appear to have no problem with self-esteem. He exerts control over his victims by catching them off guard. Rather than alerting their suspicions, he comes across as a person that can be trusted. John Norman Collins, who murdered a series of co-eds in the Ypsilanti-Ann Arbor area of Michigan, actually played upon the public's fear of a killer at large when he offered several trusting women a 'safe' ride home. These killers are so self-confident that they exhibit features of Narcissistic Personality Disorder. By itself, the disorder is far from dangerous. But in combination with the compulsion to kill, it can prove exceedingly difficult to mediate. In rare cases, the diagnosis of a personality disorder can progress to such a careless extreme that the person completely isolates himself from meaningful contact with others. The killer has evolved to a dangerous level of antisocial behaviour. The Evolutionary Model of Serial Murder is frightening indeed. This designation is used to identify a killer who is both self-sufficient and self-seeking: the need for a social environment no longer exists.

Both sets of killers display a remarkable ability to objectify their victims. In other words, victims are not considered to be people. Such objectification is not uncommon. Consider what homicide detectives and medical students must do when performing their tasks. Cadavers are shaved in an attempt to depersonalise them. Accident victims are referred to by their causes of death, rather than their first and last names. The military uses terms such as 'collateral damage' and 'friendly fire' to soften the impact on the public, and in particular the victims' families, whenever individuals are killed unintentionally. Serial killers also dehumanise their victims, which is perhaps why so many of them continue to deny responsibility for murdering people.

Serial killers are difficult to categorise, but the following theories are helpful in determining some of their salient characteristics:

Low Self-Esteem

Overt Presentation:
1. The Offence Cycle
2. Fantasy-Addiction Model
3. Medical Model

Covert Presentation:
1. Narcissistic Personality Theory
2. Evolutionary Model

2. THE OFFENCE CYCLE

The Offence Cycle Theory offers a logical approach to identifying and interpreting the actions of a serial killer. Although these murders appear random and senseless, there is a method to the madness. The model was originally developed for the treatment of sex offenders (Emerick, Gray, and Gray, 2001). This should come as no surprise considering the majority of serial murders are sexually motivated. The model examines a sequence of nine steps. Because it is a cycle, the sequence repeats itself and a predictable pattern is established.

The best way to apprehend a killer is to identify the idiosyncratic behaviours that accompany each step of the cycle. Because every killer is unique, his actions leave a piece of his identity at each step of the sequence. A profile can be put together from the information gathered along the way. Once the specific features of the cycle are identified, authorities can interrupt it. But far from describing what is already known from conventional wisdom and demographics, the offence cycle paints an offender-specific portrait. For example, most profilers know that the typical serial killer is generally a white male between the ages of 25 and 35 with an unstable work history. But this does little to tell us what motivates the killer to commit a series of murders. The following nine steps define the offence cycle:

1. Anticipated Rejection
2. Hurt Feelings
3. Negative Thoughts of Self
4. Unhealthy Coping
5. Deviant Fantasies
6. Grooming of a Victim
7. Commission of Offence

8. Temporary Guilt
9. Rationalisation

1. ANTICIPATED REJECTION

A fear of being rejected by others is the primary step in the cycle. Many theorists mistakenly believe that anger is the trigger. It is easy to make that assumption based on the level of brutality that is associated with most murders. But anger is never the primary emotion. The rage that enables a person to take the life of another person is only a mask that hides something more vulnerable. Anger covers fear. Imagine driving faster than the speed limit along a stretch of highway. Suddenly, a vehicle waiting at a side road pulls out in front of you. To avoid slamming into the car, you hit the brakes and skid off the road. You quickly become angry. But how did you feel during the split second that nearly ended your life? Serial killers experience fear and anxiety before substituting it with anger. It is a basic human need to build relationships. The need for acceptance, coupled with a failure to find it, leads some people to end the relationship on their own terms, rather than waiting for someone else to end it for them.

Anger and frustration are products of impaired social functioning. Obviously, the disability is apparent in social contexts, but what about the context of the family? How could a person know about this difficulty if he were in limited contact with others outside his family? Children normalise behaviour that is learned in the home. What is appropriate in one home may not be appropriate in another. Socially, many problems are not noticed until they reach a larger context. By the time a maladjusted child enters school, he may not realise that his behaviours are out of place. He may not be aware that he has any boundaries, until he bumps into someone else's. The resulting frustration will leave him feeling anxious and insecure. He suffers from an inability to engage in a mutual exchange or to build meaningful relationships; consequently, his self-esteem is shattered.

What went wrong in the family of origin? According to developmental psychology, the most likely answer is that the child did not learn how to trust others. Unbelievable as this may sound, his parents did not make themselves available to meet his basic psychological needs. He did not get fed when he was hungry. And although he cried, he did not get changed when his diaper continued to get soiled. He learned that he could not trust anyone to meet his needs. As he became older, he internalised this lesson. Since he could not accept that his parents had emotionally abandoned him, he made it his own fault. He must have done something wrong to deserve their rejection. He must not have been good enough to receive any affection.

2. HURT FEELINGS
Anticipated rejection plays havoc with a person's self-esteem. It leads to one feeling sorry for one's self. The second step of the cycle is defined by feelings of loneliness and despair. These feelings play into the role of victimisation. In other words, the offender regards *himself* as a victim. A corresponding set of behaviours accompanies this role. Victim posture, as it is called, is a very dangerous step in the offence cycle. Once a person decides that he no longer cares about what might happen to him, he behaves in a similar manner. People do not typically engage in risky behaviours when they care about their health and well-being. A remarkable insight into this stage was explained to me by Douglas Clark, the Sunset Strip Slayer. He said, 'Mass eruptive crime sprees and serial murder are a form of slow and not-quite-sure suicide.' This is a frightening revelation indeed. If a person experiences such a degree of self-pity, what does it matter if he takes his own life or opts for death by state?

3. NEGATIVE THOUGHTS OF SELF
It is difficult to explain the preceding stage without examining the one which follows it. The step identified as negative

thoughts is intimately tied to the feelings that cause them. Thought distortions are where the troubling projections begin. They are also the point of departure between *overt* and *covert* expressions of diminished self-esteem. The overt offender wallows in self-pity, while the covert one compensates for his negative perception by believing that it is everyone else's fault. For example, he believes that the problem would not exist if others could recognise and acknowledge his talents and attributes. In other words, they are jealous of him. But this distinction will be further explained in an upcoming chapter. The easiest motivations to recognise are the ones most obviously associated with the offence cycle, and these are the motivations of the overtly guided killer. His negative thoughts of self guide him to believe that he has nothing to lose. If he has lost everything already, what more does he have to worry about? It is dangerous thinking.

All of us have felt bad about ourselves at one time or another, but it generally manifests itself in a number of innocuous ways. Self-destructive thoughts are not uncommon. Suicidal ideation and high-risk behaviour sometimes accompany these thoughts. Excessive drinking, promiscuity, and fighting can all be defined as self-defeating behaviours. Likewise, isolation and emotional distance are also high-risk. Most of us are more likely to entertain thoughts of harming ourselves than to genuinely consider causing serious harm to others. But what if a person entertains both thoughts simultaneously? Neither one of them is truly rational, but that does not necessarily imply that they are uncommon. The way a person copes with destructive thoughts is a point of departure between *normal* irrational behaviour and *abnormal* irrational behaviour. Both forms of behaviour follow a pattern. It is difficult to predict outcomes, but it is possible to assess a potential level of dangerousness. The next step represents the earliest observable 'action' phase of the cycle.

4. UNHEALTHY COPING

In the preceding steps, thoughts and feelings characterise the hidden motivations of the offender. He may disclose them to someone else, but it is unlikely. He does not wish to appear vulnerable, nor does he trust anyone. So unless he tells someone else about them, the primary motivations for his behaviour may not be immediately apparent. What is observable, however, is his choice of unhealthy coping mechanisms. He may dabble in some of the common forms, such as substance abuse and isolation, but he may also develop some very abnormal obsessions.

Jeffrey Dahmer is a fitting example. He cited his fear of abandonment as the primary force behind his first kill. By murdering the victim, he was able to prevent him from leaving. Dahmer could not cope with thoughts and feelings of rejection. It was this inability that led to a self-medicating behaviour of excessive drinking. Dahmer himself said that he purposely got drunk before killing and dismembering his victims. He was not motivated by the act of killing itself. Instead, he killed to collect his victims' body parts. In a sick and twisted, yet literal way, he managed to keep a part of them for himself. Dahmer exhibited some very abnormal methods of coping with rejection, as well as some of the more common and normal ones. While excessive consumption of alcohol certainly clouds a person's clarity, it does not necessarily precipitate murder. The intent to murder is the product of a more ominous coping mechanism. It is a threat turned outwards. This type of unhealthy coping gives rise to deviant fantasies.

5. DEVIANT FANTASIES

Deviant fantasies are what fuel the killer. In his own mind, he becomes what he has always wanted to be. The elusive role becomes attainable. He is no longer the object of rejection that triggered the cycle to begin with. At this point, it is important to understand why the serial killer is trying to fulfil the desired role. Is he doing it for attention, power and control, revenge, or an assumed disability? These are the four motivations that underlie all maladaptive behaviour. The motivations, however, can be interrelated. For example, a killer who is seeking revenge for cruel and abusive treatment suffered during childhood is also exercising power and control over victims. Perhaps these victims represent the very person who harmed him.

Such is the case with Glen Rogers or Edmund Emil Kemper III. Rogers killed women who had the same general appearance as his mother, a petite woman with red hair. And although Kemper's victims shared little with his mother's physical resemblance, he stopped killing and turned himself in only after eliminating her. After killing his mother vicariously through the murders of several young co-eds, he forfeited this symbolic gesture and bludgeoned her with a mallet. Two of his most unusual acts are also two of the most revealing. For one, he buried the head of at least one of his victims outside his mother's window, after positioning it in a manner suggestive of 'looking in'. And once he had committed the actual act of killing his mother, he attempted to feed her larynx down the garbage disposal because he was tired of the way she had 'bitched and screamed' at him for so many years.

The attention motive is also easy to identify. Dozens of serial killers have enjoyed the notoriety that comes from contacting the media or the investigators who are working on their cases. Many of them have attempted to inject themselves into the investigation. Others have sent letters and self-gratifying messages. Clearly the killer believes that he is finally getting the recognition he deserves.

The motivation of 'assumed disability' is perhaps the most perplexing. But in many ways, it pervades the thinking of all serial killers. In other words, if the killer believes that he is suffering from some type of problem, whether socially or interpersonally, then he is likely to perceive that it is OK for him to act inappropriately. It is a built-in excuse to offend. But it is also useful to notice what he is not getting from the transaction. For example, he gets the selfish satisfaction of knowing that his victim will never experience another man after being with him. She will have nothing further to compare him with. Therefore, he is the ultimate personification of her carnal experience. What he is not getting from the transaction is the threat of rejection. So in more ways than one, he circumvents this problem by cutting short any possibility of it. He uses the disability as an excuse: it allows him to avoid rejection. Later, he uses it to justify himself and assert that he is not responsible for his actions. Remember, most serial killers believe that *they* are the victims. For the purpose of understanding the offence cycle, it is useful to replace the phrase *assumed disability* with the word *avoidance*. After all, this motivation provides a way to avoid responsibility at both the interpersonal and intrapersonal levels.

6. GROOMING OF A VICTIM

The grooming stage of the cycle is the place where most serial killers get caught. Unfortunately, serial killers are never apprehended after their first murder. If they were, they would not be categorised as serial killers. I am confident that many would-be serial killers have been apprehended before graduating to the next degenerative level. But because the process follows a cycle, law-enforcement authorities often do not get their man until he repeats the procedure. An offender's grooming behaviour is often the first observable piece of the modus operandi puzzle. Sometimes an earlier detection can be made if authorities are familiar with the subject's unhealthy coping mechanisms. But the grooming of a victim describes the killer's selection process, and consequently it follows a predictable pattern.

While some targets are victims of opportunity, many are not. That does not mean that in the latter case opportunity is not involved; most of the time, it is. But just like anyone else, serial killers have particular preferences. In treating sex offenders, this is among the most useful information to know. It assists the treatment provider in identifying subtle clues that indicate the potential for reoffence. Certain behaviours are identified as 'seemingly unimportant decisions'. But when treating a dangerous population, nothing should be taken for granted. For example, an offender who decides that his car needs cleaning at the car wash beside the local elementary school may have selected the location because it is the nearest car wash. The fact that he is a paedophile does not mean that he is denied an opportunity to clean his car. He can justify his actions by pointing out that it was the nearest location. What he cannot justify, however, is that he placed himself in a high-risk situation. This becomes even more apparent when it is learned that he arrived at the car wash at approximately the same time as school finished for the day. This seemingly unimportant decision is in fact a grooming behaviour that places the offender in close proximity to children walking home from school. It is one example of just how easy it can be to set the stage for the commission of an offence.

Most offences are not spontaneous: they are planned. Grooming behaviours are used by serial killers to lure victims into their confidence. And if the killer is good at getting people to trust him, and his victims are not high profile, he may be able to make a long career of this practice. By preying on those who are easier to miss, such as troubled teens with a history of running away from home or prostitutes who are accustomed to mobility, he can generally avoid attracting immediate attention. But before he can get close to a potential victim, he has to manipulate the environment and lower the victim's defences. He is not likely to strike in a place that is unfamiliar to him. He will choose a place that he feels comfortable to navigate without arousing suspicion. He will survey the crowd to pick out his victim. If she appears vulnerable and accessible to him, he will approach her. A common method of victim acquisition is to offer the person drugs and alcohol or money. If the victim is susceptible to this ploy, she will either come up missing or surface as next week's headline. If no one notices her immediate disappearance, the killer risks little chance of detection.

It should be mentioned that some killers employ more sophisticated methods of grooming. This can prove particularly challenging for law-enforcement officials who pursue them. Robert Berdella, for example, was a well-respected Kansas City business owner. He spent a great deal of time volunteering at youth organisations and neighborhood crime-watch programmes. He even 'took in' several wayward young men, offering them employment at his store. While this allowed him to enjoy a reputation beyond reproach, it also provided a ready pool of accessible victims. At the same time that police were uncovering evidence of his crimes, many people accused them of framing him. His compensatory behaviours were impeccably portrayed, and his grooming activities were well disguised.

7. COMMISSION OF OFFENCE

The commission of the offence is self-explanatory. The method a killer uses is a product of the earlier stages. Since these acts of murder are not random, neither are the methods – they are deliberate in the way that they are planned and executed. The ability to interpret how and why they were committed can yield valuable insights into the identity of the perpetrator. Since any series of crimes exists within a certain framework, it is useful to define the parameters. Was a certain type of victim selected? What were the circumstances surrounding the murder? For instance, was the crime committed at the same location at which the body was discovered, or was it deposited at a dump site that was remote from the area where the murder took place? What about the physical environment? Was it chosen by the killer because of an intimate familiarity with it? How much time did he spend in the actual execution of the murder? Does evidence suggest sexual assault or penetration? Were any of these acts committed post-mortem? The list goes on and on. For each question that is answered, the potential pool of suspects gets easier to navigate.

Consider what can be learned about the killer if the victim exhibits any indication of post-mortem sexual assault. The authorities would be best advised to look for a man who is hypersensitive and embarrassed of his inadequate sexual performance. Such a man would want to control all the physical variables of these experiences. He would also be inclined to have practised his need for domination in an effort to prove his manhood. He could have a record for sexual offences against children because of his perception that their lack of experience poses little threat to his manhood. But he is also likely to have picked up prostitutes for the purpose of 'practising' his virility. Investigators who interview local prostitutes might be able to determine if any particular clients have demonstrated a marked degree of performance anxiety or expressed any unusual demands for exercising dominance and control.

8. TEMPORARY GUILT

Serial killers objectify their victims in an effort to dehumanise them. But in contradiction to the popular belief that they do not have a conscience, the offence cycle shows that they do experience temporary feelings of shame and guilt. After all, these guys have felt sorry for themselves all their lives. But experiencing guilt is different from acknowledging it. Acknowledgement would make them feel even weaker than they felt in the first place. And worse yet, an acknowledgement to another person would be like turning themselves in: self-preservation prohibits it. But to anyone who thinks that the serial killer does not have an ability to feel remorse, imagine how much less dangerous such a person would be.

The person who kills without any trace of a conscience would be fairly easy to recognise. After all, his inability to exercise any meaningful restraint would be his undoing. Consider the case of Richard Trenton Chase, who was mentioned earlier. Once the Sacramento Police Department realised that a serial killer was prowling the neighbourhood, he was arrested the very next day.

Making no effort to hide or even to change his blood-soaked clothes, he was fairly easy to find. The typical serial killer certainly has an idea that what he is doing is wrong. If he didn't, he would not go to such great lengths to hide it. And if he made no effort to disguise his behaviour, he would be much easier to apprehend. It is tempting to suggest that he does not have a conscience because that gives us permission to dehumanise him in much the same way that he has dehumanised others. But such temptation underestimates the dangerousness of these individuals. It is precisely their ability to tell right from wrong that makes them so dangerous. For once the transitory sorrow they feel for a victim gets displaced, they begin to rationalise the offence. The displacement feeds back to an earlier stage of the cycle and they begin to feel sorry for themselves all over again. Only now, they feel even sorrier for themselves because of what they have done. And at no point is a person more dangerous than when he feels so sorry for himself that he no longer cares about his actions.

9. RATIONALISATION

In order to deal with these feelings of guilt, he rationalises his behaviour. He may tell himself that he will not kill again, but then he must justify why he did it in the first place. Since he could not possibly have killed without a legitimate reason, something must have driven him to commit the act. Once again, he becomes the victim. As long as he is able to maintain that belief, he has found a convenient way to rationalise his crime.

Rationalisation is the last step in the offence cycle. Literally defined, it is the offender's answer to why he killed in the first place. It is what he tells himself to make it OK in his mind. He can justify his actions. Even worse, he can justify doing the same thing again. He killed because society drove him to it. He killed because he had been wronged and no one cared. He killed because he was on a mission to cleanse the world of evil. He did not kill *good* people. Perhaps he convinces himself that those he killed were not people at all. One of the most astonishing things that many serial killers will say is that they did not kill anybody. Imagine the mental gymnastics they must have gone through in order to make such a claim. It is not a question of whether or not they are expert liars (we already know that), but what is remarkable is that many of them actually believe that they are innocent. If given a polygraph examination, some of them would pass it: not because they are expert liars, but because they actually believe their own version of events. They have told their stories so many times that they genuinely believe that they are the victims.

The offence cycle follows a pattern of predictable behaviour. Because the pattern gets repeated, it is possible to analyse and interrupt it, and such is the method by which many serial killers have been caught. In the next chapter, the repetitious pattern of a specific serial killer will be examined, and this, along with the following case study, demonstrates how the offence cycle can be used to interpret the crime of serial murder.

3. EUGENE V. BRITT, MAN-MADE MONSTER

In 1995, the dirty industrial city of Gary, Indiana was the scene of at least 127 homicides. This did nothing to improve the image of the nation's third fastest-declining city. With so many of its factories and steel mills already shut down, the city's resident population was pulling up stakes. But many could not afford to join the migration. For the multitude of remaining residents, prospects were bleak. Entrepreneurs of the gang world replaced the steel barons of decades past. Crime, unemployment and drugs defined the new culture. For those who could not escape these desperate conditions, a new form of terror emerged. Sexual predators and other violent offenders roamed the streets with alarming regularity. While this was certainly no different from the problems faced in other metropolitan areas, Gary's situation was exacerbated by an alarming inequity in its division of services to its African-American residents.

When the bodies of no fewer than six women had been found raped and strangled in several remote places within the same general vicinity, the calling card of a serial killer should have been recognised. The victims ranged in ages from 14 to 51, and all but one of them were black. It was not until the killer sexually assaulted and strangled an eight-year-old white girl in the neighbouring city of Portage that authorities stepped up their efforts to catch him. It is difficult to comprehend how a killer with an IQ of less than 70 was able to commit such a series of violent sexual assaults and murders without being captured earlier.

Eugene Victor Britt was born on 4 November 1957. He was the second of six children born to his father and mother (three older siblings were also in the home, each one belonging to a different father). Eugene's father, Elmer Britt Sr, was employed at one of the local steel mills, a job that offered a comparatively better wage than many of the other jobs available to a black man at the time. But while money was seldom a problem for the large family, infidelity and domestic violence were. At the age of five, Eugene stumbled on his mother having sex with another man while his father was at work. When she noticed him watching, she chased him from the room. Afterwards, she offered him cookies and candy to keep quiet about it. But it was not long before Eugene learned another indelible lesson about sex. While hiding in his parents' bedroom closet, he witnessed his mother being brutally assaulted by his father. In his own words: 'It was a violent act, my mother cried and screamed as my father raped her while her hands was tied to the bed post. This act was repeated almost every night and God forgive me I sat there and masturbated through it all.'

Britt had already associated sex with violence before engaging in any sexual encounters of his own. He included his three youngest sisters among his earliest encounters. By the age of fifteen, he and his sisters 'used to get beat senseless' by their parents 'for messing with each other sexually'. At that point, he decided to move out because he had grown tired of the beatings, some of which were inflicted with an electrical cord. He also stated, 'I didn't want to carry this thing between me and my sisters any farther, I didn't want to hurt them sexually, so I moved out.' It is also worth noting that Britt's relationship with his father was never genial. As Britt later said, 'My father rejected me. The reason why is because I wasn't nothing like my brothers. They are good-looking. I was the opposite. Oh yeah, don't let me forget, they all had good-looking women and girlfriends. And to make matters worse, my father always told me I'll never be nothing in life.'

But rejection by his father was not the only thing that injured him. His inability to form romantic relationships was also greatly impaired. As he said, 'I was never in love. All the girls I wanted rejected me.' It was not long before he began to use force. During one of his earliest assaults, the victim played along and set him up. After grabbing her from a deserted street and pulling her down into the basement of the nearest abandoned house, she surprised him by remaining calm. In his words, 'This girl was acting like we was boyfriend and girlfriend and that kind of eased my rage.' After raping her, he explained, 'I felt so much love. She led me around like a dog on a leash.' They walked through an alley where she pointed out her house and said that she wanted him to meet her family. He agreed to wait for her in the backyard, while she went in to get them. Minutes later, they came out with knives and pipes and gave chase. Reflecting on why he fell for the set-up, he said it was 'because I so desperately needed to be loved after all the rejections I got from girls in my neighborhood'.

After moving out of his family's home, he took up residence with a 30-year-old woman named Shelly Hall. He remembered it as an unstable environment: 'She sold drugs out [of] her apartment and had thirteen women whoring for her, and on the side she was a stripper at a club called White Eagle Hall.' As his appetite for sex continued to grow, he prowled the east side of Gary and admitted later to committing dozens of rapes. His obsession brought only temporary relief from his feelings of frustration and inadequacy. His thoughts betrayed the rage he was beginning to feel and the addiction that was consuming him. He supplemented this addiction with a growing collection of pornography. To use his words, 'I couldn't stop masturbating to save my life.' This unhelpful method of coping gave rise to disturbing fantasies, some of which continue to obsess him to this day. As evidenced by some of the self-stimulating corre-spondences that I have received from him, rehabilitation is not an option.

As his behaviour grew more obsessive, he adopted more predatory caution. But he also took increasingly bigger risks.

While holding down a job at Clark's Oil, he spent the majority of his earnings to feed his addiction. In addition to pornography, he subsisted on a steady diet of marijuana, Mad Dog 20/20 and junk food. As he suffered from the same diabetic condition that eventually killed his father, these habits contributed physiological stress to an already deteriorating mental state. After spending the majority of a summer day watching pornographic movies, he was no longer satisfied with fantasy, and went out looking for a woman to satisfy his urges. He later gave the following description of that day:

> It was my day off, so I went looking for women after I watched a porno movie. Walking on 21st, I crossed Grant into a quiet neighborhood. From there I walked through some weeds into an almost abandoned street. Coming toward me was a young girl wearing a summer dress. She looks to be 17 years old. The sun was shining. There wasn't a soul around. Pulling her off the sidewalk by her neck, she fought me as we fell to the ground. Beating her senseless with my hands, she calmed down and gave me some. She never made a sound, she just stared at me with this blank expression on her face. Pulling up my pants, I was exhausted. She wore this beautiful ring on her finger, I took it off and left. I felt strange when I was walking back home with that girl's ring on my finger.

His strange instinct proved well founded. The girl spotted him two weeks later while he was at work, and police officers surrounded the gas station. On his way to the police station, one of the officers said, 'Take that ring off his finger, that's evidence.' He was 20 years old at the time, but the state waited until he turned 21 to prosecute him. He remarked, 'I never had a chance. That ring I took from her convicted me. I never had a juvenile record, that was my first offense and I was sent to prison to do 30 years.' It is interesting to note that he blamed the ring for putting him in jail, rather than acknowledging his crime as the reason he landed there. It is a typical method of rationalisation, which career criminals often use to avoid responsibility for their actions.

Britt served 15 of his 30 years. While prison did nothing to rehabilitate him, it did teach him to become a more effective predator. He explained, 'My sexual behavior didn't change. Three years after masturbating to porno magazines and sexual movies that the prison showed across our TV screens, I took my sexual frustrations out on the prison inmates. The ones that came willingly, I didn't hurt them, but the ones who resist, I took them by force.' Motivated by a need to feel in control, his fantasy life took on a decidedly more aggressive manifestation. By the time he was released, he was more dangerous than ever.

He searched the streets for victims of opportunity. The predatory behaviours he displayed did not entail a great deal of sophistication. He preferred to stalk his victims from the shadows of abandoned buildings and tall weeds. Once they were within striking distance, he would grab them by their necks and drag them to a relatively isolated place nearby. He had selected the locations carefully, in order to minimise his chances of being detected during an assault. This method is consistent with his negative perception of himself: lacking in confidence, he preferred the element of surprise. He had failed in previous attempts to disguise his intentions. Once he approached one of his victims directly, he recalled:

I saw a girl walking alone. To cut her off, I took this narrow road before crossing the tracks. Coming off the road, I rode my bike fast along the train track. The weeds along the track was tall, so I got off my bike and pushed it the rest of the way. Hiding my bike a couple feet from the main road, I walk out on the street breathing real hard. The woman never suspected nothing. As she was passing by me, I said, 'where you going?' A car passed by us. When it was gone, she sensed something was wrong, so I wrestled her to the grass off the road. I drag her struggling deep in the weeds until I came to an opening. By her neck, I force her on the ground. Snatching her green pants off, I went for her panties. She held on to them so I couldn't take them off. That piss me off! No matter how hard I hit her, she wouldn't let the panties go. Putting my hand around her throat I applied pressure that was so great. She released the panties and went into unconsciousness. Knowing time was against me, I raped her with her panties still on. Then she start moaning and coming to. When she became aware of her surrounding, I choked her into unconsciousness. I had thoughts about prison. After that, I strangle her to death because she saw me. Gathering up her clothes, I drug her body to another area to hide her. This was the first murder and I raped her again before I rode my bike to work.

The experience heightened his anxiety. Not only did he feel that he could not approach victims without arousing suspicion, but he also strengthened the resolve that he would not go back to prison. He explained, 'The ones that saw my face are no longer here because I didn't want to go back. The ones that didn't look at me, they live, I let them go.' The most important lesson that prison taught him was to make sure that he did not get caught. Now he would kill the majority of his victims to avoid going back.

Like most serial killers, he was not driven by the act of murder itself. Instead he was driven by the fantasies that precipitated the act. He wanted attention. He wanted to feel powerful. He also wanted revenge against those he felt would not acknowledge him. For a person with such low self-esteem, it became a self-perpetuating cycle. His method of grooming victims was simple, as was his method of killing them. It would be tempting to suggest that crude methods reveal a simple mind. And while this is true in this case, there is more to it than that. Low intelligence is not a prerequisite for murder; indeed, the majority of serial killers possess high intelligence. Killing is the product of a rich fantasy life. The more sophisticated a killer's intelligence, the more sophisticated the planning and execution of his murders. But it is still his deviant fantasy that drives the act. In Britt's case, he felt a misguided sense of control when he raped and strangled victims. Rejection was not possible; it never entered the picture while he was the one controlling the environment.

The murders of his victims were straightforward. Authorities found no evidence of additional mutilation to the bodies, aside from post-mortem sexual penetration. Such a discovery is indicative of an offender who is significantly lacking in self-confidence. While this quality is common to the entire group of serial killers, such a killer would be more likely to exhibit outward manifestations of his disability. The mask he would use to disguise his social anxiety would be fairly transparent. In Britt's case, he had aroused enough suspicion from his manager at Hardee's restaurant for her to contact the police and report him as a potential suspect. And despite the risk involved, he returned to some of the murder sites for purposes of self-arousal. He recalled one such visit:

A day later I came back to that same area out of curiosity. What I saw made me cover my nose and turn away. The odor was terrible. Everything on her body was still there. Her head, arms, breasts, upper body and legs, but her [vagina] was gone. She was laying on her back when I left. Sometime during the night a animal came and ate her [vagina] off her body just to get to her insides. I got the hell out of there after that.

Unlike some killers, the sight of physical mutilation and dismemberment did not stimulate him. He left the scene and rode his bike to work.

After committing a series of eight murders on the east side of Gary, Britt sexually assaulted and strangled eight-year-old Sarah Lynn Paulsen. She had been riding her bike in a church parking lot. Her body was found in the wooded area nearby, not far from her Portage home. When asked about the murder, he confided:

> I can't talk about that incident that sent me back to prison because I feel so ashamed for what I done. But I'll say this, the death sentence was on my head for what I done. But the family of the victim didn't believe in it, so they had the state drop it. After that, I was the one who came forth and said in a plea bargain to give me life and a 100 years and that's what they gave me.

The story of Eugene Britt did not end with his apprehension. While investigating Britt for the murder of Sarah Paulsen, the police had no solid leads on the series of murders that had taken place on the east side of Gary. Britt confessed to these murders, and told police where to find an additional body that they were unaware of. Searching a wooded lot behind a vacant restaurant on US 20, police found the body of a woman that was too decomposed to determine a cause of death. His confession came as a surprise, as no one had linked him to any of the previous murders. It would be an oversimplification to say that he wanted attention for these murders; on the contrary, he could not live with what he had done.

He initially confessed the murders to Reverend Clyde Smith, who persuaded him to come forward to the police. His conscience had been punishing him. Smith ran the homeless shelter where he was living at the time. It was here that Britt adopted a fundamentalist belief in Christianity. He would later criticise Smith for not offering any further spiritual assistance. He stated:

The reason why Reverend Clyde Smith was my friend is because he wanted the reward money for getting me arrested, 89 thousand dollars. When I was convicted and sent to Michigan City Prison, I never heard from him again. Reverend Smith should know better than to glory in his self for getting me off the street. Romans 14:7 says none of us lives to himself alone and none of us dies to himself alone. If I were him, I will be scare to death if I read Romans 11:18–21.

His attorney, Gojko Kasich, has another take on why he confessed. He explained that Britt wanted to receive the death penalty. This is consistent with letters that I have received from him. Of two previous attempts at suicide, he wrote:

I couldn't understand this feeling of guilt I had inside of me. They was so intense I start thinking suicidal. Then I carried it out. I start drinking a fifth of liquor, three 40 ounces, then I smoked a bag of weed and down over a handful of sleeping pills. Stumbling in this old abanden building on the east side, I gather up all these hangers and made a wire rope. I was in the bathroom of this building. After running the wire around my neck and the iron bars in the window, once I had it secured, I set down hanging myself. After feeling the intense pressure on my neck, I black out! I thought I was gone, but something woke me back up. I start throwing up real bad, three times like someone was pumping out my stomach. I had to get out of there. It was dark outside and the night air felt good on my face. I was drunk and disorderly. Walking north I made it to the south shore train track. I start walking east toward Miller. As I was just about in Miller, a train was coming toward me really fasted. I leeped in front of it. When it hit me, I spinned in mid-air and my right leg was ripped open by the train iron stairs and the impack sent me away from the train. I was in a daze but I was conscience. The pain had my blood pressure so high I thought I was going to have a heart attack. I was shaking all over. My right leg had swole up two sides bigger and I saw all the damage inside because it was ripped open. When my heart calmed down, I crawled in these tall weeds as the train was hit it's emergency brakes. Once I was buried in these weeds, I heard two voice calling out to me. They said, if you alive say something. They repeated this, but I remain quiet. When they didn't get no respond from me, they left to report the incident. Crawlin out from the weeds, I got in a crouch position and lift myself up on my left legs and start hopping toward the toad road. I wasn't done killing myself. When I got to the fence separating me from the toad road, I got my damaged leg over first, then as I was bringing my other leg up I heard someone say remove yourself from the fence. When I turned around I saw 13 Gary Police pointing there guns at me, then I black out from shock. If Gary inforcement hadn't stop me, I would had thrown myself in front of a car or truck coming down the toad road.

To this day, he walks with a cane. He is on a lock-down mental health unit for the sick and disabled. The fact that they allow him to carry a cane demonstrates both the extent of his injuries and the low level of risk he currently poses. He spends a great deal of time composing lyrics to his own gospel songs, but he still wishes to die. The temporary guilt phase of the offence cycle has been long-term for him. It is rare for a serial killer to accept responsibility for his actions without attempting to make excuses or justifications for them. In his words, 'I have no excuse for what I done. The truth of the matter is I'm a sick man. I just want sex. I'm addicted. It's on my mind 24-7.' And that is how he rationalises his behaviour. He admits that he is dangerous and should never be allowed back on the streets.

At the time that he was free to kill, he rationalised that he had to commit murder so that he would not get caught. Rather than reach the conclusion that he would be safe if he did not commit rape, he insisted that he had to kill to protect his behaviour. Like any addiction, there is nothing rational about it. Although he would like to face lethal injection for his crimes, the government has ruled that the death penalty is cruel and unusual punishment for the mentally retarded. At the time of writing, Eugene Britt awaits transfer to Logansport State Hospital, where he will be placed in a psychiatric unit for the criminally insane.

4. JEROME HENRY BRUDOS, THE LUST KILLER

The Willamette Valley in Northern Oregon is famous for its highly prized vineyards. Nourished by healthy rivers and trout streams containing native species of cut-throat, its fertile banks produce the coveted grape that is renowned for its elegant and earthy Pinot Noir. But in the summer of 1970, the peaceful river produced the missing body of Jan Whitney, a 23-year-old student from the University of Oregon in Eugene. She had been missing for nearly two years. A family picnic along the banks of the river was abruptly interrupted by the grisly discovery.

She was where he had said they would find her. Jerry Brudos had told investigators that he had deposited the body in the Willamette River, but up until that point it had not been found. Two of the others had been previously discovered in the Long Tom River, a tributary of the Willamette. The corpses were not fully intact, but that had little to do with the processes of nature. Brudos had taken souvenirs from his victims. He had removed the breasts from two of them, and sawed off the foot of another. What type of madness had driven this killer to commit such murderous mutilation? The answers are buried deep within his troubled psyche.

Jerome Henry Brudos was born to an overbearing and emotionally cold mother. His father was complaisant and withdrawn, with a history of moving from one unskilled job to another. Jerry was the second of two sons. His older brother, Larry, was clearly favoured by their mother. While these ingredients provide a common recipe for emotional disturbance, it is seldom clear which direction it will take. In Jerry's case, the course became disturbing indeed.

It began with a fetish for women's shoes. At the age of five, he was exploring a local junkyard when he happened upon a pair of women's high heels. Transfixed by their slender carriage and revealing lines, he brought the shoes home to observe them more closely. When his mother caught him in possession of them, she was outraged. Perhaps it was because he was wearing them at the time. She displayed so much aversion to the heels, which were completely unlike the conservative attire she preferred to wear, that young Jerry realised that he had discovered a covert manner of getting back at his mother. Whether he had found a way to rattle her cage for the attention she characteristically denied him, or secretly delighted in keeping something hidden from her, he knew that he had discovered something psychologically valuable. He never destroyed the shoes, as she had instructed him to do.

Developmentally, a child should have already mastered the stage of autonomy by the age of five. But Jerry was constantly made to feel ashamed by his mother, and by the time he entered the next stage of psychological development, his feelings of inferiority had engulfed his sense of initiative. With such a predisposition, he would lack confidence and retreat into a world of fantasy. His immaturity might be well masked at the exterior level, but it would inevitably be revealed to anyone who came to know him. Beneath the quiet and calm surface lurked an abused creature. He had learned to trust no one, and his feelings of hopelessness were mounting.

Interestingly, Jerome Brudos presents a physical character that is incongruent with the public's perception of a serial killer. He is large, but dumpy. His reddish blond hair is beginning to recede and lose its colour, but the unmistakable freckles still adorn his pudgy cheeks. His eyelids hang lazily at the edges, which give the appearance of drowsiness. A benign smile and soft expression make him appear just that, benign and soft. In short, he does not pose a threatening picture. A mama's-boy appearance may be what enabled him to approach his victims without raising alarm. But to Jerry Brudos, such an analogy is insulting. In fact, his mother insisted that he take up residence in the shed whenever his brother returned home from college to claim the bedroom. His feelings of disdained impotence only multiplied when his father refused to stand up for him. Most likely, he was reluctant to contradict his wife, which would have resulted in unmitigated chastisement. Whatever the circumstances, Jerome Brudos felt utterly powerless, until he found a way to act out his fantasies of control over the opposite sex.

It began with fantasies of bondage and control. Perhaps he could dig a hole in the hill beside his house, where he could keep a live hostage. She would be his sex slave. He could dress and photograph her any way he pleased. Never mind that it was an impractical idea – he was only sixteen. He began construction on the project, fuelled by the petty theft of a neighbour girl's undergarments. Would she become the captive for whom he was digging his secret cave?

Earlier, he had taken things from the sister of a friend. He and the brother would enter her bedroom and steal the brassières and panties from her chest of drawers. But that no longer aroused him. He had graduated to taking things from clothes-lines in the neighbourhood, a daring enough manoeuvre, considering he might have been seen. Without the added protection of an accomplice to stand lookout, it was a very real possibility. But as with all reinforcing behaviours, he was successful at it. Soon he would dare to enter bedrooms at night, while the occupants slept obliviously in the same room. It was during one of these episodes that he first formulated the idea to acquire a captive.

The hole in the hill was exhausting work, and even he realised that it seemed a bit farfetched. He would devise a more practical, albeit slightly more fanciful scheme. He had found the ideal victim. She was an eighteen-year-old neighbour whose bedroom he had entered while she slept. Because he had taken her underwear and been particularly aroused by her choice in lingerie, he felt compelled to approach her several days later. He waited until the opportunity presented itself for him to catch her alone in the yard. He explained that he was working with the local authorities, helping them find the person who was responsible for the theft of several women's undergarments in the neighbourhood. He attempted to ease her scepticism by insisting that he was an inconspicuous aid because of his residence nearby. It is doubtful that she truly believed him, but she had no reason to fear him. He seemed a pathetic teenager with little more than an active imagination.

On the night of his decision to follow through with the execution of his plan, he phoned the neighbour girl and told her that he had a lead, then asked her to meet him at his house. It was an odd request, but he seemed harmless enough. No one was there to greet her at the door when she arrived. When she knocked, a voice called from within the house, instructing her to come in. She hesitated, then brushed off her apprehension. She entered the front door. The voice called again from upstairs. She did as she was told. Jerry waited until she had reached the top of the stairs, then jumped out at her, waving a cruel-looking knife. He was wearing a mask, though it did little to disguise his identity. He ordered her to remove all her clothes. With a knife to her throat, she had little recourse but to comply.

She fumbled with her buttons, which seemed the only reasonable form of protest against a powerful captor who showed no sign of softening his resolve. Following his directive, she disrobed. He positioned her in various poses and photographed her. Once the film was finished, he left the room. She quickly retrieved her clothes and got dressed. On her way towards the stairs, she encountered Jerry again, this time without the mask. He told her that someone had broken into the house and that he had been locked in the barn, but that he had then freed himself and chased off the intruder. Fearing more trouble to come, the girl excused herself. Amazingly, he let her pass. She was too frightened and embarrassed to tell the authorities what had happened, and decided it was better just to avoid Jerry Brudos altogether.

But Jerome Brudos had revealed another secret about himself – his obsession with photography. In addition to stealing mementoes, such a person would be likely to document his crimes on film. It was a fact that would later prove vital to his criminal convictions. But for the time being, Brudos was simply adding to his treasure-trove of artifacts from which he could gratify his escalating need for arousal.

The following year, Brudos's obsession would become more physical. He lured a seventeen-year-old girl into his car and drove her to an isolated location, near an abandoned farmhouse. It may be difficult to comprehend how a potential victim could have been so trusting, but Brudos had perfected his approach. His compensatory behaviours and grooming techniques were quite disarming. After all, he was just a big, goofy kid who did not appear to know his way around the block. But quite the reverse was true – he did know what he was doing, and since he could not find a girl to give consent, he would find some other means to touch a girl for the first time.

He dragged the girl from the car and proceeded to beat her. These were not the loving, tender touches that most pubescent boys fantasise about. Instead, young Brudos was enacting his unmitigated rage against a world that he perceived had rejected him. What he could not have by consent, he would take by force.

Fortunately, the abandoned farmhouse was not the only structure on that deserted road. A couple that lived down the road were returning from town. They observed what was happening and pulled over, then demanded that the two of them get in their car. They took Jerry to the police station, while the girl received medical attention at the local hospital. She had suffered extensive bruising and a broken nose. Confronted with the undeniable facts of his brutality, Jerry was committed to Oregon State Hospital for a psychiatric evaluation and a subsequently determined length of stay. It was here that he was given an initial diagnosis.

Psychiatrists determined that Jerry Brudos suffered from an adjustment disorder, specifically related to problems with adolescence, and that he displayed features of sexual deviation and fetishism. But adjustment disorders are not pervasive, and so their assessment of his dangerousness had missed the mark. It was believed that he would recover from the fantasies. After eight months, he was released with the recommendation to 'grow up'.

The latter part of his diagnosis revealed what was really going on. Fetishism is a chronic addiction. It is characterised by arousal from non-living objects, such as women's undergarments and shoes. The urges produced by the possessor's fantasies cause 'significant impairment in social, occupational, or other important areas of functioning' (American Psychiatric Association, 1994). His fetishist paraphernalia would continue to grow, until it included such macabre objects as human breasts and feet, which he removed from the bodies of later victims. At this time, he would also develop a taste for necrophilia. But for the time being, a misdiagnosis would enable him to roam freely, continuing to escalate in his deviant behaviours.

Once released, he continued to prowl the neighbourhood bedrooms at night, searching for new pieces of clothing to add to his collection. But there was more. He began actively searching for stimulating objects during broad daylight. For example, he noticed an attractive woman wearing a red dress and decided to follow her down the street. As she turned to enter her apartment building, he seized her by the throat. He choked her into a semiconscious state, then made off with her shoes. Clearly the cycle was beginning to heat up.

The reinforcement schedule demanded another assault. Fuelled by the success of his previous attack, he gained confidence. With what he imagined to be great stealth, he pursued another woman. Only this time, the would-be victim fought back, and he was able to grab only one shoe. Maybe this was not going to be as easy as he thought it would be. But Jerry firmly believed that just because his goals were unaccomplished didn't mean the idea itself was bad. The failure was simply due to a lack of careful planning. Next time, he would be more cautious.

To ensure a greater probability of success, he returned to his old habits. Earlier in the day, he had followed an attractive girl wearing sexy shoes. He found out where she lived, then waited until nightfall, entered her bedroom and found her asleep, as expected. But what he did not expect was that she would wake up. Fearing she would scream, he choked her into unconsciousness. And then it occurred to him – she was his to do with as he pleased. Her limp body aroused him. He raped her, then left with her shoes. Although his earlier crimes had been sexual in nature, it was the first time that he had attempted intercourse with a victim. He was now more dangerous than ever.

In the meantime, he had managed to hide behind a façade of normality. He met a naïve seventeen-year-old girl named Darcie. At 23 years of age, he was looked upon as a suitable provider. She would have done just about anything to escape the humdrum condition of living at home under her parents' strict rules and expectations. So when she became pregnant with Jerry's child, she had managed her escape. But marriage to Jerry was anything but normal.

Darcie became a living model for Jerry's fantasies. He insisted on complete nudity whenever they were not in the public eye. The one exception, of course, was a pair of black patent-leather spike-heeled shoes. She complained about how uncomfortable the shoes felt, but it was not her decision to make. She had also learned it was pointless to protest against his avid picture-taking. It seemed that Jerry had an excuse for everything. He told her that the photographs would never leave their home. In fact, he would develop them in his own darkroom, adjacent to the back of their garage. He made all the rules. But if there was one area in which he was forced to admit his own ignorance, it was the bond between a mother and child. Darcie insisted on a change in the rules when their infant daughter became a toddler. No longer would they parade through the house without clothing.

Another peculiar proclivity was his fascination with wearing women's undergarments. Not that he did it very often, but once was more than enough for Darcie's innocent upbringing. She thought he must have meant it as a joke on each of the rare occasions that she witnessed it.

By and large they got along well, but the marriage became increasingly strained. It evolved to a point where they both occupied the same house, but would go about their separate business. He spent most of his time in the workshop in the garage, while she visited friends as often as she could. Jerry's relationship with his daughter was not any better. He was distant towards her, as he had never learned to bond with females. They were the object of both his obsession and rage. When Darcie became pregnant with a second child, she barred him from the delivery room. He was not allowed to witness the birth of his own son. This was a crushing blow to an already fragile ego, and Darcie and Jerry became very distant, like strangers towards one another.

Rejection shattered him. But he had a method of coping with such things. He would make himself feel better by pursuing familiar habits. Only this time, he would intensify his behaviours. The fantasies had become more violent, and he would take control by acting them out. Armed with a psychological purpose, he had become a very dangerous and deliberate predator.

The first to die was a victim of chance. Linda Slawson was nineteen years old. It was a blustery January day and the sleet was coming down in sheets. She was the only person to be out on such a difficult day, when all other sensible people were snug in their homes. But she had encyclopedias to sell, and maybe a house along the thoroughfare would make the endeavour worthwhile. She was surprised to see a large man tinkering with an automobile outside his garage. She approached him. Maybe he was interested in buying a set of books for his kid. Judging by the tricycle in the yard, this was a family man. Jerome Brudos lured the young woman behind the house and down into the basement. He seemed interested in what she had to say about the books. A basement seemed an odd place to discuss the terms of sale, but Brudos explained that his mother was upstairs babysitting the children and that he wanted the purchase to be a surprise. Besides, any place that was dry would be a welcome reprieve from the miserable weather.

Once she entered his private domain, he knew that she must never leave. His pulse raced as he realised that the fantasy of securing a captive had become a reality. He picked up a loose piece of lumber and smacked her over the head with it. She fell instantly. Although she was unlikely to regain consciousness, he had to be sure. He wrapped his heavy hands around her throat and squeezed until he was certain she was dead. Although he had murdered an attractive young woman, he was not seized by panic. Sure, it was brutal, but he was amazed by the clarity of his thoughts. As long as the incident remained undetected, he could do with her as he pleased. Her body now belonged to him.

His brain was functioning at an acute level of awareness. So acute, in fact, that he decided to do something quite normal. He went upstairs and offered his mother five dollars to pick up some burgers from a local fast-food restaurant. She left and he returned to the basement. Minutes later, another potential interruption presented itself. Heavy footsteps sounded on the floor above him, accompanied by a familiar voice. A friend had stopped by to see him. Not wanting to risk detection, he decided it would be too risky to allow him to wander through the house. What if he searched the basement? Brudos exited from the back door, then came around to the front of the house. Pretending to be coming in from outdoors, he greeted his friend with the excuse that he was out in the shop working with nitroglycerine. That seemed to deter him, and the friend left after making arrangements to meet him later.

Brudos returned to the basement. She was still there, waiting for him. He undressed her, and then, treating her like a life-sized doll, he dressed her with articles of clothing from his own secret collection. It was difficult to select a favourite set of undergarments. He wanted to remember her in all of them. He retrieved his camera, but it was out of film. He berated himself for being so stupid, and resolved never to make that mistake again. But time was running out. He wanted to hang on to his prize, but he knew that he could not keep her forever. It was too risky. And besides, the body would be too impractical to try to preserve.

Perhaps if he could not keep her, he could take a souvenir. Her brassière and panties would have significant meaning, but he already had an ample collection of those types of things. Besides, this was different. It was his first kill. It did not seem appropriate to take a manufactured article of clothing. He needed something more personal and intimate. It was then that the idea occurred to him. It was like an epiphany. He would keep her foot.

Using a hacksaw, he severed the foot from the rest of the body. Now he had something he could fit in the freezer. He would keep it locked and tell his wife not to bother with anything inside. If she needed something from the freezer, she could contact him through the intercom and he would retrieve it for her. It seemed like a good plan, but he would still have to dispose of the rest of her body at the earliest chance.

Later that evening, he formulated a plan. He would dispose of the young woman's body in the Willamette River. He drove to the St John Bridge. Even though it was two o'clock in the morning, traffic could still be expected. He would have to act quickly, and with deliberation. And then a brilliant ruse came to him. He would pretend to have a flat tyre. That would give him ample time to carry the body, weighted with an engine head, to the side of the car that was obstructed from view. The beauty of the plan was that nobody ever stopped to help a stranger in need. In fact, they would be certain not to even look at him for fear of having to offer some form of automotive assistance. The entire plan went off without a hitch.

Returning to his basement, he regarded the trophy that was all his. Adorning it with various spike-heeled shoes, he was pleased with the artistic specimen. He satisfied himself until it was no longer feasible to hang on to it. And then he had to get rid of it. He attached a weight and sent it beneath the Willamette.

The cycle had completed itself. For a short while, Jerome Brudos had known what it felt like to be in complete and total control. He had tasted omnipotence and its effect was intoxicating. But it was not long before the familiar feelings began to return. He was physically powerful, of that he was certain. Why then did others not recognise his superior qualities? He continued to feel awkward around women, who seemed to regard him as not worthy of a passing glance. Revenge swelled in his mind. If others could not see his true power, he would make them take notice.

Although the fantasies were always present now, he had not decided on the best way to convert them to reality. Consequently, he had not chosen to stalk a particular victim. He went about his daily business, but the feelings of inadequacy were mounting. There was only one way to alleviate those feelings. He maintained a vigilant lookout and, as luck would have it, another victim of opportunity presented herself.

Jan Whitney could not figure out what was wrong with her car. It was very late and she was unlikely to expect help alongside the I-5 freeway at such an inconvenient hour. Depending on the kindness of a stranger left her in a vulnerable position, but the man who had stopped seemed harmless enough. His freckled face and gentle features seemed to suggest an affability not unlike the friendly clerk at a neighbourhood hardware store. And he knew something about cars. When he explained that she would be unable to start it without the proper tools, she felt dejected. He said that he could fix it for her and invited her to jump in beside him, while he went home to retrieve his toolbox. When she hesitated, he insisted that she would be safer with him than she would be alongside the road.

He drove her to his house on Center Street, and she waited in the car while he went inside to get his tools. He returned with the toolbox, opening the back door on the passenger side of the car. But in addition to bringing the necessary tools, he had brought an additional one. Before she could turn to see what he was doing back there, he looped a broad leather strap over her head and squeezed it tightly against her throat. She died with a minimum expenditure of effort on his part. He was getting good at this. Now that the difficult part was over, he could indulge in his fanciful games. But this time, he would do more than just play dress up with her.

Generalised revenge and a desire to shame the victim governed his next move. Overcome with an urge to intensify the intimacy of his act, he turned the body over and sexually penetrated it from behind. Next, he suspended the body from a rope in his workshop. For several days, he left her there. He returned often to dress her in various articles of clothing and to engage in necrophilia, all the while photographing his handiwork. Soon he would have to dispose of his toy, but not without first taking a souvenir.

While secretly deciding what to keep, he continued to live the outward appearance of a humble family man. He drove his family to Portland, so that they could spend Thanksgiving with the in-laws. He was not one to panic. The fact that a dead body was suspended in his garage did not cause any degree of alarm. On the contrary, the very thought that he was able to pull one over on the rest of the world was simply a testimony of his cunning. He felt more powerful than ever.

But as poetic justice would have it, a drunk driver careened off the road and slammed into the corner of his garage while they were away. It left a substantial hole in the wall of his workshop, which was noticeable immediately upon his return. A wave of panic now surged through his being. It was inconceivable that the dead girl had tried to escape, but the shock was greater than he could bear. How could someone else have known what he had been up to? He hurried his wife and children indoors, then went over to inspect the damage. A business card indicated that the police had been there to make a report. They must have tried to gain entry to the garage, but the door was locked. He hurriedly unlocked it. She was still there. He temporarily blocked the hole with a makeshift obstacle, and lowered the body to the floor. He wrapped it in a plastic tarp and carried it to the pump house. Making sure that no suspicious or incriminating evidence was left behind, he phoned the number on the card. The police arrived to take a report, which he would need to get an assessment of the damage for insurance purposes. Although he was nervous, he played it cool. It was all very routine. They had not noticed anything out of the ordinary. His superior intellect had kept him in control of the situation. But still, he would have to act quickly now to dispose of the body.

Discarding the first one in the Willamette River had been easy, so he knew where to take the body of Jan Whitney. But he still had one problem to solve. What would he take from her before she disappeared forever from his life? Surveying the body once more, it came to him. Her breasts would make a nice set of paperweights. At least, that is what he later told authorities. The truth might have been more disturbing. He removed one of the breasts and scraped the inside clean. Then he stretched it over a mound of sawdust and tacked the edges to a board. Another killer who had engaged in similar activities was Ed Gein. He used erogenous parts and genitalia to construct a female body suit, which he wore to complete his transformation. Given Brudos's propensity to dress in women's attire, it is likely that he attempted to assume a feminine identity. Women were incorrectly identified as the weaker sex. What many of them lacked in physical strength, they made up for in psychological supremacy. Although he could demonstrate excessive physical force, his entire life had been dominated by the unwavering authority of women. A breast was a token of this power. What better item with which to stuff his brassière than an authentic human breast?

He drove to the Willamette and executed the final step in his commission of the offence. He pushed her mutilated corpse, weighted with a piece of scrap iron from his pump house, over the side of the bridge. She would not be found until nearly two years later, and the body of his first victim, Linda Slawson, would never be found.

Had the police caught him with the body of Jan Whitney suspended from a rope in his garage, there would have been no more murders. But they had not observed the body when they left their card at his home, following the accidental damage of his garage. The authorities had no reason to suspect that a serial killer was operating in their midst. The disappearances of Linda Slawson and Jan Whitney were being treated as missing persons cases. But a more isolated dump site would reveal the truth. For the time being, Jerome Brudos was free to kill again. And this time, he would actively stalk his victims.

The next to die would be Karen Sprinker. Brudos was cruising the streets of Salem on the morning of 27 March. Not certain what he was looking for, he knew that he would recognise it when he found it. It was ten o'clock when he discovered the perfect woman to satisfy his deviant fantasy. She was dressed in a mini-skirt and high heels. He quickly found a space in the parking structure and returned to follow her into the department store. He searched the store for over an hour, but could not locate her. Returning to his car, he spotted another woman. She was more plainly dressed, but she happened to be in the right place at the wrong time.

He approached Sprinker with a replica toy pistol. Thrusting it towards her, he explained that he would shoot if she screamed. She felt she had no choice but to comply. He took her to his car. She begged for her life, reasoning that she would do anything he asked, as long as he did not kill her. Back in Brudos's garage, he raped her. Afterwards, he handed her a pair of lacy panties and a fancy brassière. Instructing her to put them on, he took pictures of her in several different poses. The humiliation was nothing compared to what came next.

Tying her hands behind her back, he explained that she would have to be restrained to keep her from running away. Could it be true that he was going to spare her life? Would he leave her unattended for a short period of time, during which she might be able to devise a plan of escape? It was a false hope, indeed. He placed a rope around her neck, attached to a come-along. Swinging the loose end over the hoist, he gave a tug until the slack was taken up. He asked if it was too tight. When she cried that it was, he cruelly cranked the come-along until it lifted her off the floor. Her legs kicked and her body began to twitch. He watched callously as she suffocated to death.

In a supreme demonstration of his confidence and self-control, he went inside to spend some time with his family. Later that evening, he returned to the workshop and had sex with the corpse. More professional now, he knew what to do with his trophy. He cut off her breasts and packaged her up to be taken to a dump site. He even thought to dress her in an oversized bra stuffed with paper towels, so that she would not bleed on the seat of his car.

If he was going to continue these activities, he had to find an alternative dump site, just in case any of the bodies were discovered. He did not want to be in any way connected to the earlier site at the Willamette River. What if someone could place him at the location on either of the nights the bodies were dumped? People might have been generally stupid, but they were funny that way. For some reason, they tended to remember what was normally considered ordinary in the context of something extraordinary. Besides, he had a better dumpsite in mind. Not only was it more isolated, it was also more intimate. He was much more familiar with it than anyone else was likely to be.

As a child, he had wandered along the secluded banks of the Long Tom River. If he took her to the disused bridge on Irish Bend Road, he could complete his ritual in secrecy. Nobody would interrupt him while he made preparations to dispose of the body in the gentle waters of the Long Tom. After tying the body to a cylinder head, he tossed it into the river.

Like most serial killers, he was a creature of habit. He operated within a very particular zone of comfort, and needed more than cursory control over his environment. As such, he lured victims or took them by force to his workshop. As a base of operations, it was a place where he had collected all the tools of his trade. He was comfortable to act freely in these familiar surroundings. It was a place where he could control all the variables. It is doubtful that he would have committed murders away from his homemade torture chamber, unless he had been able to expand operations to another familiar setting. A need to meet such conditions is probably the reason that he met with only limited success.

Before he took his fourth and final victim, there were numerous failed attempts to lure others to their deaths. The most notable was that of Sharon Wood. As he attempted to abduct her from the parking structure at Portland State University, she fought back. Why did so many of them fight back? He had tried to perfect his grooming procedure, favouring the darkened interiors of parking garages and rendering his would-be victims more vulnerable with a replica toy pistol, but this one had inflicted injury upon him.

He had only just managed to get one arm around her neck and the other in front of her face when she bit him. He had tried to muffle her screams with his free hand, but she clamped down on his thumb. As she had punctured the flesh, he had no choice but to slam her against the concrete. He promised to make her pay for this audacious opposition, but he would not get the chance. A Volkswagen Bug came around the corner and chased him off.

It was not that his plan had been an imperfect one. In fact, he was confident that it was flawless. It was just that he had selected the wrong victim. He did not perceive that he was capable of making a mistake, but he needed to be extra careful. Anyone who got away might be able to describe him.

Incredibly, a similar incident happened the following day. A girl from Parrish Junior High School was walking alongside the railroad tracks when he spotted her. He got out of his car and hurriedly made his way towards her, then grabbed her by the jacket and dragged her between two buildings. He pulled the toy gun on her and demanded that she come with him. As he directed her towards the car, she broke and ran. When she made it to the safety of a neighbour's yard, he dared not follow her. Instead, he retreated to the car and left the scene as quickly as possible. The only way to erase the failures would be to ensure that the next abduction was a perfect success. But the recent string of errors had come with a hefty price. The latest escapee had been able to provide police with a physical description – and the modus operandi seemed to fit with at least one another attempted kidnapping.

Time was running out for Jerome Henry Brudos. But it would not expire before claiming another victim. Linda Salee was a petite woman of 22 years. She was returning to her car on the sixth floor of the parking garage at the Lloyd Center shopping mall. Carrying an armful of purchases, she was in a vulnerable position from which to try to defend herself. And he was in no mood to greet another failure. He flashed a fake badge and asked her to come with him. She demanded to know what for. He explained that she had been caught shoplifting on surveillance camera. She protested, but he was unwavering. Anxious to clear the matter with mall authorities, she irritably went along. By the time they reached his car, it was obvious that something was not right. But by then, there was no choice but to comply.

After forcing her into the car at gunpoint, he drove the hour's distance to his home in Salem. He parked the car inside his garage and tied her securely with a length of rope. No one knows precisely what happened next. Brudos asserts that he left her there, while joining his family for dinner inside the house. It is quite possible that this is true. If so, it is a clear indication that his behaviours were escalating in both their level of sophistication and cruelty. If not, it signifies the beginning of the end of his mind, in which fantasy blurred the boundaries of reality. In either case, there is little doubt about what happened immediately afterwards.

He strangled her with a leather strap and sexually penetrated her dying body. Afterwards, he suspended her from a hook in the ceiling and attempted to reanimate the body with electric shocks. He attached wire leads to a pair of hypodermic needles and inserted them in her ribcage. It didn't work. Instead of making the body twitch, it burned her flesh at both points of entry. He sexually penetrated the corpse again, then carried it to his car. He was not going to keep this one any longer. Of all his victims, she was the only one that he left anatomically intact. When asked about that, he explained that her body did not interest him very much. The nipples blended together with the rest of her breasts. The specimens were not perfect enough to meet his purpose. He attached an automobile-engine part to the body and disposed of it in his favourite dump site, the Long Tom River.

An escalation of the cycle was not apparent in the post-mortem treatment of the body, which showed no dissection or severing mutilation, but it was present in the commission of the offence. Brudos engaged in sexual penetration at the moment of execution. Perhaps he was becoming addicted to the act of killing. Maybe he was no longer satisfied with merely collecting his trophies. As a means to an end, murder was one thing. It was a necessary step in the acquisition of objects to gratify his sexual urges. But in the murder of Linda Salee, there was something more: a growing need for the object of fantasy to take on a consensual role. To the normal person, nothing in Salee's victimisation suggests consent. But to the psychopathic mind, having sexual possession of her at the moment of death provides the illusion of consent; and the attachment of electrodes to the body suggests an attempt to prolong this experience.

Jerome Brudos was beginning to demonstrate his pathology in the signature pattern of his killings. Authorities recognised that they were looking for a man with the psychological disposition of an abandoned child. He was likely to be awkward and immature around women. If this was the same man who had attempted previous abductions from city parking structures, such as were known to have occurred in the Sprinker and Salee cases, then they also knew something of his physical appearance. He was a large man with soft features, fair-haired and pale with light-coloured eyes. Then came the break they were searching for.

Still too awkward to approach women in a direct and congenial manner, he began using the telephone. Utilising a college campus directory, he phoned several girls and attempted to introduce himself by saying that he had got their numbers from a friend. It did not usually work. But for every few failures, he was rewarded with a success. One young woman agreed to meet him. She was a student at Oregon State University, the same school that Karen Sprinker had attended.

In a canvass of the area, officers were assigned to speak with residents of Karen's dormitory. One of them happened to be the girl that Brudos had recently contacted. Although she had no idea that the man she had gone out for a Coke with was Oregon's most wanted, she did remember an odd comment that he had made. Upon returning her to the dormitory, he asked why she had agreed to come with him. He then inquired how she could have been certain that he was not going to take her to the river and strangle her. After she repeated this to the officer, she was asked for his physical description. It seemed to match the description given by Sharon Wood and the girl at the train tracks. The freckles that had once coloured him harmless were now the mark of a wanted man.

His comment to the girl at the dormitory revealed three further characteristics of his pathology. First, it suggested his arousal in sensing the fear that he could create by talking about the bodies found in the river. It was a fear that betrayed a young woman's trust in men, and perhaps he could capitalise on that. Secondly, it demonstrated the power he had to control life and death. By suggesting that he could have killed her, then allowing her to live, he was hinting at his own imagined omnipotence. And finally, he was rationalising his prior offences by convincing himself that he could make up for them by 'saving' her from harm. He even went so far as to educate her about the most effective method of self-defence. He told her to kick an attacker in the shins, insisting that a shot to the groin might throw the defender off balance.

But try as he might to win her favour, the content of his message had raised alarm. Suspecting that he might contact her again, authorities asked her to agree to meet him the next time he called. Of course, they would be on hand if such a date were ever scheduled. Eleven days after their first meeting, he called again. She made arrangements to meet him, and phoned the police. They picked him up in the downstairs lobby of the dormitory. The cycle of Jerome Henry Brudos had come to an abrupt stop.

After his arrest, he was booked at the Salem City Police Station. When he was given a pair of jail coveralls, processing officers were amused to find that he was wearing an oversized pair of women's panties. His embarrassed explanation was that he had sensitive skin.

Like most serial killers, he believed himself superior to other human beings – not just in the case of victims, but also with regard to the authorities. This feature will be made more apparent in the upcoming chapters on narcissistic personality theory and the evolutionary model. Piles of physical evidence were collected from his workshop. Fibre analyses were conducted on the ropes and rug found there. Witnesses who knew him to be in possession of specific automotive parts had been able to identify them to police before knowledge of their origin had been made public. These were the same parts that had been used as weights on some of his victims. Confronted with a hefty body of evidence, he continued to maintain that as long as he failed to provide the right answers, he could not be directly linked to any of the crimes. In fact, he told investigators that his IQ was 166, just in case they failed to recognise that they were dealing with a superior intellect. Later evaluations revealed a score of 105. It is possible that stress impacted these results, but a discrepancy of more than sixty points is highly unlikely to result solely from this. In other words, Jerry Brudos imagined himself to be far more intelligent than he truly was.

Only one thing worried him. Now that he was in custody, he could not get home to properly dispose of his cache of incriminating photographs, undergarments and shoes. Perhaps he could get word to Darcie to destroy them. She had been greatly distressed since his arrest. An obedient wife, she did not deserve to get dragged into this. It was a difficult decision, but self-preservation demanded it. He phoned her with instructions to enter the workshop that had once been considered off limits. But she did not comply. While it was true that he had exerted total control and dominance over their relationship, the tide had shifted. It was not that she wanted to incriminate him. If anything, she hoped for the sake of her family that he would not be found guilty of the charges. But common sense told her not to get involved any further. Guilt by association was hard enough. Besides, if he had done nothing wrong, he should not have anything to worry about. On the other hand, if reports in the media about his suspected activities were right, she wanted as little to do with him as possible.

Investigators found the incriminating items. Among them was a photograph in which he had inadvertently identified himself. A naked female body was suspended by a rope. Underneath, a mirror had been positioned to reflect the image of the vagina. Ever the skilled photographer, he had manipulated the subject to capture it from two different angles. But in the heat of creative expression, he had accidentally photographed himself. Captured in the reflection of the mirror and preserved in the image of the photograph, a significant portion of his face was clearly visible. Confronted with irrefutable proof, he told authorities everything that had happened.

Jerome Brudos was given three life sentences. Each sentence carried a minimum of twelve years. Authorities never found the body of his first victim, Linda Slawson. Given the accelerated rate of the Willamette's turbulent currents and the passage of time, it is doubtful that she will ever be found. Sent to the Oregon State Penitentiary in 1969, he is eligible for parole in 2005. Although he has been a model prisoner, it is doubtful that he will ever be released.

His actions are clearly traceable to the offence cycle. He admitted to killing his victims, but he rationalised his behaviour according to a series of innocuous medical diagnoses. He claimed that hypoglycemia, exacerbated by an unhealthy diet, is responsible for his actions. If low blood sugar could be identified as a cause for murder, then the world would indeed be a far more dangerous place. His psychological addictions provide the best explanation for his behaviours. In fact, he continues to accumulate magazines and catalogues that feature women's shoes. Since mail is not censored at Oregon State Penitentiary, it is easy for him to acquire the images for his obsession. Obsessions fuel the fantasy. And just as powerful as any psychotropic substance, the addiction to fantasy is what drives the offence cycle.

5. THE FANTASY-ADDICTION MODEL OF SERIAL MURDER

It has recently become widely accepted as fact by law enforcement and other authorities who are concerned with the study of serial murder that fantasy plays a significant role in both the life and motivation of the serial murderer. However, what is not so widely held is that fantasy is utilised by the serial killer as a coping mechanism to assist his day-to-day survival. Another point, which is still being considered, is that, like the alcoholic, the serial killer is also an addict. The obsession to commit murder is so strong that the serial killer commits the act in order to preserve his addiction, which he considers to be his only means of survival.

We can no longer think of addiction as being simply pharmacological. It must now be considered as a bio-psycho-social disease, which is not an isolated illness but contains components of psychology, biology, and sociology.

The bio-behavioural approach to addiction applies both to the individual and the biological segments of the addiction, and, because it reveals these to the analyst, it can be viewed as an extension of the bio-psycho-social theory of addiction. As is already known, addiction can be defined as the repeated use of a substance or an obsessive involvement in a behaviour, which, in some way, modifies the psychological and physical identity in a manner that produces harmful, long-range effects for the addict. The object of the addiction is used to comfort the addict. The addict believes, rightly or wrongly, that the substance he is addicted to possesses some magical power, which provides him with the necessary tools to function on a day-to-day basis. The substance, in reality, has no actual effect on the anxiety itself, but this is a realisation that the serial killer is incapable of making. The appeal of the addiction is best understood when we understand the medicating power that the addictive substance has for the addict.

Addiction is, like most other debilitating and life-threatening diseases, progressive. The progression rate is based within the individual addict himself. Addiction builds cumulatively, until the addict is destroyed by the addiction or a resulting side effect.

Hypersexuality is also an addiction, particularly when it is of the type exhibited by such serial killers as Ted Bundy and Jeffrey Dahmer. Sexual addiction is a mood altering experience in the same way that heroin or cocaine addiction is mood altering. Like all addictions, sexual addiction is a progressive cycle. Gradually, the addict focuses his attention more and more on sex. The sexual behaviour is a psychotropic agent. Over time, the sexual behaviour increases and leads to altered cognitive states, as a result of the increase.

As a psychotropic substance, sexual behaviour is utilised as a coping mechanism. Engaging in sexual activity allows the addict to feel better for a limited period of time. It is this brief period of freedom from feelings of low self-esteem that leads directly to the addiction to sexual behaviour.

Numerous theories propose that in certain individuals the neurotransmitter level in their brain predisposes them towards a variety of distinct addictions. These theories attempt to link the genetic basis for an addiction with an overall genetic predisposition. There are, however, additional biological factors which influence the choice of addiction. For example, if an individual becomes physically ill upon the ingestion of tobacco, he is unlikely to become addicted to tobacco and will seek another substance to become addicted to, something that does not make him sick.

Beyond any genetic or inborn disposition to addiction, there are similarities in the backgrounds of all addicts. One of these is the difficulty in establishing interpersonal relationships, which we find in addicts of all types. Another similarity is that addicts tend to come from homes with high levels of conflict existing between the parents. Poor parenting and the lack or total absence of tactile stimulation, which leads to antisocial behaviour, is yet another similarity discovered in the backgrounds of all addicts. In addition, addicts perform poorly in school, have no sense of purpose or direction in their lives, and are often underachievers. They avoid responsibility and suffer from both depression and low self-esteem. All addicts have difficulty in controlling their behaviour.

Sexual addiction can be classified as a continuous compulsion for sexual stimulation accompanied by an unnatural and unwarranted high level of self-hatred. Sexual addicts are often hyperactive, have a short attention span, and are prone to aggression when their needs for stimulation are not met. The self-hatred experienced by the sexual addict causes him to seek ways in which he can increase his self-esteem. He chooses to gain power through the act of sex.

As was mentioned earlier, there are predispositions to different types of addiction. The addiction that is chosen is influenced by many factors. These include heredity, availability, and the influences of family and society on the individual. All addictions are sequential in nature and can be seen as evolving in three distinct stages. The first stage occurs when the individual undergoes an experience that leaves him inclined toward addiction. The second stage is marked by the individual utilising the addiction as such, and the final stage occurs when the addiction has progressed to the level of compulsion. The length of each stage in the addiction process is the sole variable in the equation. This depends on the individual and is influenced by his attitudinal precursors, as well as the external stresses experienced by him.

The addiction is utilised to gain self-esteem, but in the process the existing self-esteem is damaged even further. The individual has no other choice but to continue the addiction in order to achieve a normal level of self-worth. The term addiction does not apply in the use of the substance to alleviate certain emotions and feelings, but rather when it is used as the sole method of dealing with negative emotions.

The onset of addiction is marked by a noticeable change in the use of the addictive substance. When focus shifts from using the substance for recreation to using it for coping, the usage and need for the substance is reinforced. The progression of the addiction is determined by its reinforcement.

The serial murderer is a sexual addict of the highest and worst degree. He is incapable of loving anyone and is also incapable of developing any lasting relationships, if they do not have some sort of cause and effect value for him. He is impulsive, calculating, and extremely prone to violence. He is constantly in search of new thrills and does not make the effort to control his own behaviour.

Serial killers are inherent sadists who are fascinated with violence and pain. They fantasise about causing injury and torturing their victims. These individuals feel no guilt, but possess strong feelings of severe insecurity and general anger towards all others. All the traits that help normal people cope with the stresses of daily life fail to develop in these individuals.

The serial killer commits his crimes for purely psychological gain. There is always some sexual component to these crimes. He is motivated by the need to meet his desire for sex; to fulfil his addiction. The crimes are always pre-planned, because fantasised violence is part of the addiction.

Serial killers may be classified according to several distinct models, which were defined in Chapter One. This chapter introduces a further division, that of process-focused versus act-focused killers (Holmes and DeBurger, 1988). The killers classified as process-focused utilise excessive violence and overkill, and indulge in activities with the dead body. These individuals kill for the thrill of it. They have no interest in having a dead body on their hands, other than to fantasise about power and control over it. Danny Rolling was a process-focused killer. He positioned his victims' bodies for maximum shock effect, then left them to be discovered in these disturbing poses. Upon entering the apartment of one of his victims, police found the woman's head propped on a bookshelf, while her decapitated body was sitting at the end of her bed. Her nipples were also found on the bed beside her. And to add further shock and horror, investigators attempting to move the body discovered that it had been sliced from the breastbone to the pubic bone.

The act-focused killer, on the other hand, commits his crime quickly. He kills in order to see the end product of his work and to collect the trophies of his labour. The act-focused killer murders his victims only as a necessary side effect of his other activities with the body, which are what he actually enjoys the most. He often keeps parts of victims' bodies for masturbatory purposes. Jerome Henry Brudos was an act-focused killer. He kept a woman's foot in the freezer, from which he often retrieved it to place in various high-heeled shoes. He took several photographs of this 'trophy'.

Fantasy is the driving element in the life of the serial killer. Elements of the fantasy are observable at the crime scene and within the murder itself. The fantasy intrudes upon the thought patterns of the killer, which are already distorted and incite him to murder. His addiction eliminates his recognition of society's values and he kills over and over again. Elements of the fantasy can be seen in the condition of the body, as well as its positioning and disposal. The killer uses his victim as a prop to recreate his sadistic fantasies.

The first murder committed by a serial killer is an experience of euphoric physical and psychological arousal. Pleasure is taken over the control the killer has over his victim. Murder is a psychological high. The extreme cruelty which the killer imposes upon his victim excites him to a state of sexual arousal.

To further fuel the need to kill, the serial murderer relies on his psychopathological desire for risk. These individuals rely on the adventure and thrill that taking risks provides, and with each successful murder, the killer begins to feel as if he is invincible and will never be stopped. This leads to the taking of bigger risks, which leads in turn to the making of mistakes and, eventually, apprehension.

The basis for fantasy is laid down in the childhood of the serial killer. As a result of poor family life, abuse, neglect, and increased feelings of isolation, the killer retreats deeper and deeper into a world of dark fantasy where he is, at last, in control. Though no single factor has been proven to cause serial murderers to emerge in our society, childhood abuse is one factor that can be directly linked to the origination of a fantasy world. This abuse causes physical, psychological, and sexual arousal and leads to the creation of fantasies which link sex with violence. The only way for these individuals to become sexually aroused is through the use of violence.

Sexually sadistic fantasies in childhood not only serve to alleviate a child's fear, but also serve as an outlet for the massive amount of pent-up hostility and aggression he feels towards the people who have abused him. Once used as a form of escape from an abusive and neglectful home life, the fantasy soon becomes a substitute for the child's ability to control his feelings and emotions, which leads to addiction.

As the child grows older, the function of the fantasy expands to other areas of his life. The fantasy finally becomes the only source of arousal for him and serves as the fuel for the commission of later, violent crimes. Precursors to serial murder include cruelty to animals, fire-starting, and aggressive behaviour. These behaviours and others are the child's attempt to try out and practise his fantasies. As he grows older, these fantasies turn to murder.

The fantasy totally encompasses the adult addict. It serves as a replacement for control and emotions, and the feelings of failure which plague all serial offenders. Since fantasy plays such a dominant role in the serial killer's life, it has eliminated any and all personality traits of a positive nature that the killer had the potential to develop. As a result, what remains are negative traits which include autoeroticism, fetishism, dishonesty, disdain for others, and aggression.

This reliance on fantasy also blurs the distinction between what is real and what is not. Resulting from this distortion in perception and the negative personality characteristics of the serial killer, he is unable to connect to other people and to form stable, normal relationships with the rest of the world.

The fantasy itself is the primary cause of the feelings of isolation the serial killer experiences. This isolation leads to self-hatred and to anger against the world. This in turn serves to provoke violent acts, which lead to greater isolation and, therefore, greater reliance on fantasy. It is a vicious, self-destructive, self-perpetuating cycle, which thrusts the future serial killer further and further outside the realm of what society deems to be normal. This cycle is similar to that of other addicts, such as alcoholics and drug abusers.

One of the central problems the serial killer experiences is the total inability to distinguish between degrees of violence, or recognise what constitutes proportionate violence. He is incapable of toning down his actions to suit the situation or challenge he faces.

The preference serial killers have for autoerotic behaviour, such as masturbation, is a result of their inability to form normal, lasting relationships. They have no other choice but to seek ways in which they can satisfy their sexual urges independently. There is, in this instance, the need for visual stimuli, which is why there is a need for a victim.

The serial killer is unable to anticipate any positive outcomes surfacing from his behaviour. These attributes are absent in the fantasy. Fantasy becomes a place where the serial killer is always in control. It is an alternate reality, which for the serial killer is real. As the last remaining coping device that the killer has, fantasy continually evolves and leads to experimentation with his victims.

With every incremental act of violence, the serial killer moves closer to the outward expression of his frustration. With each conquest, the killer gains temporary self-esteem. But as the need to recreate the fantasy and the need to preserve it intensify, the entire concept behind the initial creation of the fantasy backfires on the killer. He becomes a slave to the fantasy and is caught in a place between what is and what is imagined. It progresses to a point where the killer has to commit murder in order to have any normal emotions. At this stage, the excitement is gone and the killer must find new ways to stimulate himself.

Murder is an extension of the fantasy. It is a logical progression. Once the fantasy is acted out and murder is committed, it becomes linked to reality and leaves the killer with a sense that he can manipulate reality. The more murders the serial killer commits, the greater the psychological gain he achieves. The murders preserve and reinforce the fantasy, so the fantasy survives, as does the killer's belief that he has done nothing wrong. The feeling a serial killer gets from committing murder is so strong that he has no desire to stop. With each murder, the fantasy is also moved closer to perfection because it feeds off itself and becomes more structured, like some perverted version of the learning curve. The more murders the killer commits, the better he becomes at killing. The killer learns from the past, takes mental notes about mistakes, then analyses his plan and improves it.

The minute the serial killer commits his first murder, the fantasy grows and he needs to kill again. The time between kills also decreases as the number of victims escalates. This is because the feeling of self-worth experienced by the killer is only achieved when he kills, so he will want to have that feeling on a more regular basis.

All addicts suffer from a downward spiral as their addiction takes over. It is at this point that their entire lives centre around the substance of their addiction. The serial killer's life begins and ends with murder. The cycle of serial murder is the same as the cycle for other addicts, the only difference being that here the end result is murder.

6. HADDEN CLARK

Serial killer Hadden Irving Clark currently resides in Cellblock Four in Western Correctional Institution in Maryland. The inhabitant of cell number ten, Clark has convinced himself that he is a woman. This fantasy life in which he has immersed himself has led him to request that be be referred to as Kristen Bluefin. He also believes that there is a sixteen-year-old girl named Nicole inside him, and that she is the evil daughter of Kristen Bluefin. Clark insists that he never killed anyone, and that, in fact, the true culprits were the girls who reside within his consciousness, created by the constant and addictive activity of engaging in fantasies regarding intense sexual activity and violence. So deep and vivid is the fantasy world in which Hadden Clark exists that he urinates sitting down, flirts with all the males he comes into contact with, and bats his eyes at all those who will look at him.

Clark has expanded this fantasy world even further since his incarceration. He often acts as though one of his female personas is a hunter and there is a food shortage. He empties and scrapes his grapefruit down to the rind, fills it with whatever he has around him that is edible, and covers it with paper. He hides it in the corner of his cell until it becomes fuzzy with mould, then he eats it. At 6'2", 165 lb, Hadden Clark is not the picture of health. He shaves his head and his eyebrows, and spends his days vomiting or sitting over the toilet with diarrhoea, but denies that his dietary habits have anything to do with his rapidly deteriorating physical condition.

In the cell next to Hadden Clark is a man named John Patrick Truitt. Clark has convinced himself that Truitt is Jesus Christ. Since November 1999, Truitt has served as a confessional for Clark. Working with the FBI in exchange for a reduction in his sentence, Truitt readily pretends that he is Jesus in order to fulfil

Clark's fantasy and to extract from the serial killer the details of all his crimes, including information regarding any and all of the murders he has committed. Between 1999 and 2001, Truitt filled some 203 pages in several notebooks, documenting the statements made by Clark. There are also several pages of drawings, which Clark himself has sketched regarding his criminal activities. One of the most interesting items Truitt has extracted from Clark is that he wishes and has promised to murder his brother Geoff and Geoff's wife Alison, if he should ever be released from prison. The murders, Clark contends, would be justified because Geoff wore a wire when he once talked to Hadden in prison and Alison testified against him at his murder trial.

The fantasy world which Hadden Clark has constructed is so complex that when both he and Truitt were confined to a state mental hospital and Maryland detectives took the pair on a series of trips up Interstate 95 so that Clark could reveal where he had buried his victims, Clark refused to leave unless Truitt was allowed to go with them. He reasoned that when the bodies were located, Jesus could bring them back from the dead. Clark also demanded that he be allowed to dress like one of his female personas, down to the bra and panties. The trips were quite extensive, leading detectives all around Massachusetts, Connecticut and Pennsylvania.

Clark informed Truitt during their first days in adjoining cells that he had murdered six-year-old Michele Dorr and detailed where he had buried her, seeking forgiveness from Truitt for his sins. He explained that he had buried Dorr's body along with a bucket of several pieces of jewellery collected from his other female victims, and that the body could be found on his grandfather's property. Acting on this tip from Truitt, the FBI recovered the remains of the six-year-old, fourteen years after Clark had murdered her with a butcher knife. Thus began the relationship between Kristin Bluefin and Jesus Christ.

Hadden Irving Clark was born in October 1951 to Flavi and Hadden Clark Sr. The Clarks' second-born son was extremely aggressive as a child. He often hurt people for no reason and struck out against them physically when he did not get his own way. According to family reports, Clark was unable to tell the difference between right and wrong and lacked a conscience, as well as any sense of remorse or compassion for others. Whenever he felt wronged by others, he would kidnap their family pets, torture and murder them, and then leave their bloodied corpses on the families' doorsteps.

The Clark family believes that Hadden suffered a head injury at birth, caused by a difficult forceps delivery. As evidence for this, they point out that by the time other children his age could read and write sentences, Hadden had still not begun to talk in complete sentences. His ability to walk also suffered. At the age of four, Hadden was brought to Yale University's Child Study Center, where he was diagnosed as having cerebral palsy and mild damage to his brain.

Several key events seem to have forced Hadden Clark to retreat into a sheltered and safe world of fantasy. For one thing, his parents often engaged in violent physical altercations, stemming from verbal arguments they had regarding him. These episodes often occurred in his presence. For another, he was often left home alone, while the other Clark children were taken on camping and hunting trips. This rejection and exposure to violence led Clark to trap small animals, torture them and then murder them, all in the course of a month after they had been captured. The prolonged suffering inflicted on these creatures reveals that Clark was totally oblivious to the pain he inflicted on other creatures, and that he was methodical and willing to do whatever it took for him to gain some sort of satisfaction.

Another factor which would contribute to Clark's need for a safe haven, the kind he found in fantasies, included his father's lack of empathy for him. Clark also suffered from physical, emotional and psychological abuse at the hands of his father. Hadden Clark Sr was an alcoholic who required regular doses of lithium to control his manic depression. Hadden's mother was not much better, dressing him as a girl in pink dresses and frilly undergarments because his parents had both wanted a girl. This sort of humiliation continued until Clark was in elementary school. Additionally, his father constantly referred to Hadden as Kristen, which explains the choice of name Hadden uses to describe his alter ego, Kristen Bluefin.

Clark never outgrew his attraction to feminine clothing, and he continued to dress in women's clothing into adulthood. He was engaging in acts of voyeurism in his teens and had been sexually assaulted by his older brother Brad at about the same time. Although he reported the incident to his mother, she ignored it and the assaults continued to occur.

Unlike most serial offenders, Clark possessed below-average intelligence, as measured by the standard battery of intelligence and psychological tests administered during his time in school, as well as after his apprehension. In 1964, Clark was placed in a boarding school for the learning disabled. After three years, he achieved some level of success and returned again to the public school system.

In the early 1970s, Clark began to explore his fascination with knives. He enrolled in the Culinary Institute of America in Hyde Park, New York, where he demonstrated a talent for carving. At this time, Clark began to collect every type of kitchen knife he could get his hands on, and spent every free minute sharpening and then storing them in a long metal box. In 1974, Clark graduated from the Institute with an associate's degree. But despite his talents, Clark could not maintain a job. He switched positions fourteen times between 1974 and 1982, even though he was given the opportunity to take some of the more choice positions at several of the best restaurants in the country. His one achievement in the culinary field occurred in 1980 at the Olympics in Lake Placid, when Clark won a best-of-show ribbon for his ice sculptures.

On 31 March 1982 he violently and inexplicably attacked his mother, leaving her with several injuries. She pressed charges against him for assault, but the court in Maryland refused to prosecute the case. Following the incident, he was no longer allowed to live inside the house he shared with his mother and took to sleeping at a number of sites on the property. In 1983, despite his history of learning disabilities, Clark was allowed to join the navy. His homosexuality eventually surfaced during this time and he received frequent beatings from the other sailors. One beating in 1984 put Clark in hospital. He was examined by the navy in 1985, and was diagnosed as suffering from paranoid schizophrenia with manifestations of persecution and grandiose delusions. He was discharged with thirty per cent disability on 22 June 1985. A few days later he arrived at his brother Geoff's house in Washington, DC, where he was allowed to live in the basement. Clark was arrested two months later for shoplifting panties and brassières from a department store.

As a peculiar aside, Hadden Clark was not the only member of his family to have been arrested for murder. His brother, Brad, was charged with first-degree murder and mutilating human remains in 1985, after he murdered Trish Mak. Brad's ex-wife, Linda, reported to police that Brad had confessed to murdering three other people and mutilating their corpses, as he had done with Trish Mak. Police claimed they were too busy to investigate the allegations, and Brad Clark was never prosecuted for any additional murders.

Trouble seemed to follow Hadden Clark wherever he went. In 1986, Geoff Clark ordered his brother to move out of the house because Hadden had masturbated in the presence of Geoff's children, after skinning and mutilating rabbits in front of them. Clark moved out. In 1989 he attempted to get a job, despite the fact that he had $40,000 in his checking account. The menial jobs he could get did not last long, and he eventually went to the local veteran's hospital to seek help for his condition. His mental state was diagnosed as psychotic with questionable etiology, but he did not receive treatment because he left the facility before being officially admitted.

Out of control and not smart enough to commit the perfect murder, Hadden Clark murdered Laura Hoeghteling on 18 October 1992. Houghteling was the daughter of a woman who had taken pity on Clark and paid him to do odd jobs around her home. It was a completely premeditated homicide: Clark had purchased two rolls of duct tape, a coil of braided rope and three boxes of lime, four days before committing the crime. After midnight on 17 October, Clark pulled up in front of the Houghteling house and let himself in with the spare key he knew was located in the shed. He was wearing a wig that made him resemble Laura, panties and a bra stolen from Penny Houghteling, and women's shoes. He was also carrying a purse.

In a moment in which Clark's twisted world of fantasy became reality, he questioned Laura as to why she was sleeping in his bed and wearing his clothes. He made her call him Laura, then murdered her and placed her body in the bed of his truck. In order for Clark to survive, he had to become Laura Houghteling, and that meant that she had to die. At eight o'clock the next morning, he completed his transformation by stealing her briefcase and waiting at the bus stop where she always waited to go to work. Later, Clark would return to the truck and drive the corpse to a secluded area, where he buried it. On 21 October 1992 Clark deposited the trophies he had taken from Houghteling's room in a storage locker he had rented at Warwick's E-Z Mini Storage Compound.

As he was already a suspect in the murder of Michele Dorr, the minute Clark's name was mentioned by Penny Houghteling, police realised they had to find him. On 6 November 1992, Hadden Clark was arrested in the parking lot of the First Baptist Church in Bethesda, Maryland, for the murder of Laura Houghteling. Infuriated, the police did not read Clark his Miranda Rights, and instead took him immediately to the police station, where for the next seven-and-a-half hours Clark requested an attorney over one hundred times. His request was ignored. On 17 December 1992 he was formally indicted for first-degree murder. His trial began in June 1993. He pled guilty on 25 June and was sentenced to a term of thirty years in a maximum-security facility, despite the fact that Dr Gary Kay of Georgetown University Medical Hospital stated that he had a malfunction in the left lobe of his brain.

Hadden Clark reverted to the only form of remorse he knew when he was placed in the Eastern Correctional Institution, that of being beaten by his father. He achieved this by spitting into the coffee of other inmates, inciting them to beat him mercilessly. Eventually transferred to the Patuxent Institution, a state mental facility, for a six-month evaluation, Clark continued his self-injurious behaviour by telling anyone who would listen about how he had murdered six-year-old Michele Dorr. More beatings followed, including one which left Clark with a cracked skull that required stitches and landed him in protective custody. Several inmates also began to record Clark's confession, and this information was turned over to police.

Transferred to Roxbury Correctional Institute for further evaluation, Clark was eventually charged with the murder of Michele Dorr. He was found guilty and sentenced to another thirty years. Clark also received an additional sentence of ten years for an unrelated theft, and now faced a total of seventy years behind bars.

In addition to the crimes for which Hadden Clark is currently serving time, he is suspected of several other murders. He has been connected to the murders of Sarah Pryor and Cathy Malcomson, who disappeared in Wayland, Massachusetts, an area where Clark's father had grown up and his grandmother had died. The files of Dawn Cave, 14, Mary Mount, 10, and Doreen Vincent, 12, were also reopened by police, and their disappearances have again been linked to Hadden Clark.

There is no telling the exact number of victims Hadden Clark had over the time he spent killing. Although he has willingly confessed to some crimes to the man he believes is Jesus Christ, some of his memories have faded. He exists now in a rapidly deteriorating state, both physically and mentally. He believes that his suffering, through acts committed by his own hands, is the only way for him to atone for his sins.

The serial killer in Hadden Clark emerged very early in his life. A combination of mental illness, brain damage, abuse and genetics led him down the path of seeking shelter and solace inside the world of fantasy. It is the factor of fantasy, the complexity of it, and the reality of it, that for Clark was the turning point in his life.

He engaged in a world of fantasy in which he was a female. This fantasy world was constructed, in part, by the way in which his family treated him. In order to cope with the humiliation and abuse he suffered, Clark convinced himself that he had to become a girl, since that was what his parents had wanted him to be. His fantasy world led to the need to become the women and children he murdered. For him to have a purpose, he needed to become his victims. In order for him to consume them, identity and all, he had to kill them. It was what the fantasy required if Clark was going to survive. Without the ability to assume the identity of other women and, therefore, fulfil his fantasy, Clark has decided to give up on life and allow himself to die. The crimes of Hadden Clark constitute a horrible tale of violence and depravity, but they also represent the failings of the criminal justice system, the mental healthcare system, and the public education system to intervene in the life of someone who was clearly severely troubled for such a large portion of his life.

Interventions at any stage of Clark's life, while not a guarantee of preventing the violence that he eventually released upon society, might have provided the outlet he needed to deal with his deep feelings of inadequacy. However, the systems designed to support, identify and treat the type of problems which he had readily and openly displayed since childhood, failed to live up to their duties. This sort of failure is quite apparent when we examine the type of serial killer who most closely follows the fantasy addiction model of serial murder. The fantasy, like any other addiction, manifests itself in visible ways which advertise certain warning signs to all those involved in the life of the addicted individual. It is only when the professionals involved in the early lives of individuals who may be suffering from an addiction to unhealthy fantasy begin to recognise these warning signs that we will truly see a genuine reduction in the frequency and type of crime committed by killers like Hadden Clark.

7. JEFFREY DAHMER

Jeffrey Dahmer, a modern day cannibal and one of the nation's most infamous serial killers, was born on 21 May 1960. His parents, Lionel and Joyce Dahmer, had made a comfortable living in the modest Milwaukee suburb of West Allis. By the time he entered grade school, Dahmer had a morbid fascination with death and dismemberment, which led to one of the most blatant addictions to perverse sexual fantasies known to the study of serial homicide. The young Dahmer collected small animals, killed and dismembered them, then placed their body parts in glass jars. He did not have a uniquely distinct personality, as other children do. Rather, he would behave according to what he believed adults expected of him. His father would describe his son as a social outcast. Combined with the addiction to fantasies involving death and dismemberment, the absence of a personality and the related social difficulties manifested themselves early in Jeffrey Dahmer. They were present to such a damaging degree that he had no other choice but to act upon his fantasies, in order to restore some sort of equilibrium inside his troubled mind.

Dahmer's behaviour, both in childhood and as an adult, may have been affected by the fact that his mother was taking medication for her anxiety and depression while she was pregnant with him. These powerful sedatives may have had a negative effect on the brain, nervous system, or body chemistry of the unborn Jeffrey Dahmer. Such damage can be compared to the effects of fetal alcohol syndrome. Fetal alcohol syndrome impacts normal brain development. Victims of this syndrome are known to have poor impulse control and to engage in the creation of violent fantasies. In adulthood, people who suffer from FAS have difficulty following the rules of society and engage in violent acts because they are incapable of controlling their behaviour to conform with social expectations.

Another contributing factor in Dahmer's rise to the position of serial murderer can be seen in the tremendous difficulty he had in adjusting to his mother's second pregnancy. This event led Dahmer to feel increasingly isolated from his family and the rest of the world. He felt abandoned and fostered feelings of anger and hatred for his brother, who was born on 10 December 1966. Due to his mother's own mental health issues, the feelings of abandonment and neglect that Dahmer experienced were allowed to continue for a much longer period of time than is considered to be healthy by most child psychologists. It is common for every first child to feel a certain amount of withdrawal of their mother's love after the birth of a sibling. Most compensate, and eventually accept the sibling with a feeling of responsibility. Dahmer compensated in an unhealthy and damaging way by internally severing ties with his family, drawing his emotions inwards, and retreating to a world of fantasy. The pain that he felt was only released through the torturing of small, defenceless animals. As an adult, with these feelings never resolved, Dahmer expressed his pain and emotional torture by murdering his victims in an attempt to create zombies that would never leave him and would love him unconditionally. If he could create such loyal companions, he would never again be left feeling neglected or isolated from the world.

After an apparent episode of sexual abuse at the hands of a neighbourhood child when he was only eight years old, Jeffrey Dahmer became obsessed with cruelty towards animals and began to devise newer and more brutal methods for torturing and putting them to death. He initially began acting out his perverse fantasies by collecting insects and butterflies, then quickly escalated into collecting road kill. He would carefully and methodically perform the dismemberments in a tool shed located behind the family home. This space was ideal for such activities because it provided him with the requisite privacy, due to its remote location on the property. Dahmer also built his own graveyard near his home, where he buried the animals he had killed and marked their graves with miniature crosses he constructed from scraps of wood.

One particularly disturbing habit, which was a precursor to the way he would later torture and mutilate the bodies of his human victims, was to bury the bodies of dead squirrels in the ground and to mark their grave sites by impaling their skulls on the crosses near the graves. This habit, however, did not keep Dahmer satisfied for very long, and he had become an aggressive hunter of neighbourhood animals by the time he had reached his early teens. During this emotionally troubling and fantasy-charged time in his life, Dahmer attended Eastview Junior High School; it was at about this time that several dogs went missing from the area. One of the beloved pets was found behind Dahmer's house; its head had been made into a totem pole, and its body nailed to a tree.

Dahmer explained his obsession away as being nothing more than an interest in science. It was an excuse that Lionel Dahmer, a scientist by trade, was willing to accept. Dahmer claimed that he only dismembered the corpses of the animals because he wanted to see the way that things worked inside. Jeffrey Dahmer also enjoyed listening to people's heartbeats and touching their veins to feel the blood course through them. This was another habit that he would carry with him into adulthood and incorporate into the ritual of the brutal homicides he committed.

It is clear that Jeffrey Dahmer was a very disturbed young man. He exhibited five warning signs of deviant behaviour, which can ultimately be linked as influences in the formation of a serial killer. These five warning signs were identified by Dr Joel Norris and are as follows:

1. Parental neglect
2. Eldest or least favourite child
3. Outsider in the family

4. Ambiguous stories of childhood abuse
5. Cruelty to animals

When Jeffrey Dahmer entered high school, he was probably already sociopathic. He was bombarded by feelings of loneliness, frustration and hostility, for which he had no release or coping mechanism other than the creation of fantasies rich with violence. He never developed any of the mechanisms for dealing with conflict which are generally established in early childhood. He was an emotional basket case who was left to drown in a sea of wayward and confusing emotions by his family. Developments while he attended high school, including his parents' divorce, his chronic alcoholism, and his continued perceptions of abandonment, would firmly establish him as a serial killer later in life.

In high school, Jeffrey Dahmer was constantly either drinking or drunk. He would begin his day at 7.30 a.m. by drinking beer, which he smuggled into school inside his coat. By the time he was fifteen, Dahmer was an alcoholic who used the substance to dull the feelings of pain he was experiencing. Dahmer sailed through the cracks of the public education system. Since he was not a discipline problem, no one ever so much as questioned his strange behaviour, which included, amongst other things, drawing chalk outlines of bodies on the ground similar to those located at crime scenes.

By the time Dahmer was a senior in high school, these bizarre tricks were referred to as 'doing a Dahmer' by his peers and teachers. He acted without restraint, as the flood of alcohol swimming through his system lowered any inhibitions he might have had. Dahmer constantly acted the goat so that he would be the centre of attention. This need for attention emerged out of a nagging desire to compensate for the feelings of neglect he experienced every waking minute of his life.

Though it is not uncommon for teenagers to seek attention, it was the way that Dahmer acted and the things that he did which pointed to serious mental problems. He did not seek to be funny in order to make people laugh, but acted instead out of frustration and anger. When the old tricks no longer drew crowds or laughs, Dahmer adopted new tricks into his act. One of these new tricks was to fake an epileptic seizure in a public place.

The amount of alcohol which Dahmer drank on a daily basis was so great that he suffered from seriously impaired judgement the entire time he was in high school. This contributed to fuelling his sociopathic tendencies and caused him to withdraw from everyday life even further than he had already decided to do. One of the negative side effects of this withdrawal was Dahmer's fear of dating a girl. He attended his high school prom with a girl who was asked to go with him by a mutual friend. Dahmer was so terrified of her that he handed the corsage he had bought to her mother to pin on, rather than attempting to do it himself. He did not dance with her the entire night and he refused to kiss her when the night was through. Instead, he shook her hand after returning her safely to her house.

While it is easy to believe that Dahmer's erratic behaviour, such as the ability to be the class clown and an unnatural fear of dating, is contradictory, this is not the case. The two extremes are not mutually exclusive. Instead, they are compatible with one another. Dahmer was incapable of a one-on-one relationship, especially with a member of the opposite sex, because he felt like he was being judged and because he was socially maladjusted and inhibited. Any one-on-one confrontation rendered him helpless. When in a group, however, he was usually drunk and uninhibited, which caused him to feel like he was in control of the group. After all, his behaviour always made him the centre of attention. His attendance at the prom was a one-on-one situation. He felt threatened by it so, to be in control, he had to ignore his date. Otherwise, she would have paid too much individual attention to him.

His parents' divorce during his senior year in high school placed a great deal of additional pressure on him because he was forced to choose between the two of them. This event and the circumstances surrounding it became the focal point in Dahmer's development into a serial murderer. Dahmer's parents fought so bitterly with one another that they split the house in two and each lived in a separate part without having any contact with the other. When he turned eighteen, Dahmer became an adult in the eyes of the court, which excluded him from any settlements the divorce might render. His brother was provided for, since he was younger. Jeffrey, however, felt like he had been forever removed from the family and that there was nothing he could do about it. He felt that he had no one to help him come to terms with what was going on.

The court's ruling that Dahmer did not require parental custody led to an increased sense of abandonment. To compound this, in June 1978 both of his parents moved out of their home temporarily. They had not talked to each other about the decision. When this took place, it was unknown to either parent that Jeffrey Dahmer had been left in the house alone with no food and no money. This is significant from a developmental standpoint because most children who experience feelings of abandonment become stuck at the very age that they feel this abandonment occurred. For Dahmer, such feelings began to occur at the age of five or six. Children at this age have difficulty controlling and expressing frustration. Rage often prevents them from conforming their behaviours to the dictates of law or society. Such are the characteristics that would accompany Dahmer into adulthood.

The incident in which Dahmer was left inside the house by himself implanted in him the need for companionship like never before. This need would manifest itself in the murders that he committed, the goal of which was to create the perfect victim who would never be able to leave him. The birth of this fantasy necessitated that he would have to force someone to remain with him. It became an instant addiction that took root at the very time of his abandonment by his family. If he could only find someone who would remain with him, then and only then would his feelings of abandonment subside. He was convinced of this, and nothing would remove him from the course on which he was now headed with full steam. For Dahmer, torture, mutilation and murder were the only solutions to the problem he had wrestled with throughout his entire life.

Motivated and spurred on by this latest abandonment and the rapidly growing fantasy of permanent companionship, Jeffrey Dahmer got into his car and started upon the first active stage of serial murder, hunting for a victim to fulfil his fantasy. He came upon Steven Hicks on 25 June 1978. Hicks was hitching a ride to a concert and was a good-looking young man. Dahmer, who had experienced homosexual fantasies since he was fifteen years old and who had accepted his homosexuality fully by the time he had reached eighteen, was immediately attracted to Hicks and invited him home for some drinks. The moment that Steven Hicks stepped into Jeffrey Dahmer's car, he was as good as dead. Dahmer's homosexual fantasies, which have often been downplayed in previous studies of his crimes, had been compounded and had fused together with his other obsessions some time ago. The night that he picked up Steven Hicks, they combined with his fantasies of companionship, inciting him to act on them completely, without looking back and without regret.

The murder of Steven Hicks set the stage for the pattern which Dahmer would follow and to which he would become addicted over the course of the rest of his murderous career. The pattern was an outgrowth of Dahmer's childhood obsession with the mutilation and display of dead animals. Because the crime followed a stressful and traumatic event in Dahmer's life, it had greater significance than any of the murders he committed afterwards, and also served as the triggering mechanism for later homicides.

The murder itself did not bring a release of the feelings of anger and frustration that had built up inside him, although such a release is often the case in serial homicides. Rather, along with the consumption of alcohol, which was used during every subsequent murder and can be seen as part of the ritual of other serial murderers including Henry Lee Lucas, Ted Bundy and Arthur Shawcross, Dahmer used this murder and all his future murders to medicate himself against unwanted feelings.

Further insight into Dahmer's later murders can be obtained from a careful examination of the Steven Hicks homicide. This is especially true since Dahmer changed his story about having sex with Hicks in his numerous confessions to police about this specific crime. By telling police that he had had sex with Hicks, then denying that sexual intercourse had taken place, Dahmer illustrated that his main problem with his social functioning was the way in which he perceived homosexuality. Hicks was not homosexual, and probably rejected Dahmer's sexual advances. This rejection was a monumental blow to Dahmer's already fragile self-esteem and he was even more repulsed by his own homosexuality, which he had grown previously to embrace. It drove Steven Hicks away from him, which was the last thing in the world that Dahmer wanted to do.

In a panic reaction, Dahmer struck Hicks over the head with a dumb-bell, killing him. Since Dahmer had already developed an interconnection in his mind between sex and violence, it is likely that he became sexually aroused during the murder and more sexually attracted to the dead Steven Hicks. The murder was a horrible experience. It was the one moment in his life that Dahmer would never be able to escape from, regardless of how much alcohol he consumed.

What is even more incredible about the murder of Steven Hicks is that Jeffrey Dahmer was almost arrested for the crime. If he had been, he would never have become the notorious serial killer so familiar to us. After killing Hicks and dismembering the body, a process that took Dahmer several hours and made him physically sick, Dahmer placed the body parts into several garbage bags and piled these into the trunk of his car.

He then set off to dispose of the remains. Dahmer was pulled over for driving erratically and was issued a field sobriety test. When he passed the test, the officer allowed him to drive away with nothing more than a warning.

Obviously shaken by the near arrest, which would have put a quick end to his killing spree before it had even begun, he drove home and placed the garbage bags in the crawl space of his home. A few days later, Dahmer initially attempted to dispose of the remains by stuffing them inside a drainage pipe. This attempt was unsuccessful, so he decided to dig a grave beside the pipe, but this too was unsuccessful. He then created a shallow grave behind his house where the dirt was softer and placed the bags inside it, leaving them there for a few weeks. Realising that this method of disposal would not work for very long, Dahmer proceeded to dig up the body parts. He cut all of the remains into smaller pieces then removed the flesh from the bones, dissolved the organs and flesh in some acid and flushed the sludgy mixture down the drain. Next, he smashed all the bones into a fine powder with a sledgehammer and dispersed the dust off the top of a cliff, then buried Hicks' wallet and dumped his other possessions in the Cuyahoga River. Six weeks later, his father and his father's new fiancée returned to the house to visit Jeffrey. They moved in with him, and a few weeks later he left to attend Ohio State University. Steven Hicks' disappearance would remain a mystery for thirteen years.

Jeffrey Dahmer's obsession with alcohol followed him to college, where he stocked his dorm room with liquor and drank constantly. He spent almost all of his money during his first few weeks at school and was forced to sell his plasma in order to purchase more alcohol. He quickly became isolated from his peers, who were more serious about their academic endeavours. His father came to visit him at school and was shocked by the number of empty liquor bottles in his son's room. Disgusted by his son's behaviour, Lionel Dahmer decided that Jeffrey needed to leave college and join the military.

On 24 December 1978 Lionel Dahmer and Shari Jordan were married. On 30 December, Jeffrey Dahmer enlisted in the United States Army and was sent to Fort McClellan in Alabama on 12 January. He chose to become a military policeman, but was kicked out of the rigorous programme in May. He was then transferred to Fort Sam Houston in Texas, where he learned some of the skills he would use in the commission of future murders, being trained as a medical specialist.

Remarkably, Jeffrey Dahmer received his Military Specialist qualification and was sent to Baum Holder, West Germany, on 13 July. His bunkmates soon caught on to the secret that he was, in fact, an alcoholic. Dahmer carried a specially made briefcase that opened into a portable bar. This violation of the rules was overlooked because, initially, Dahmer performed his day job exceedingly well. His unit considered him to be an excellent medic and a respectable leader. Bunkmates reported that unlike other soldiers, Dahmer did not put pictures of his family up in his area, and nor did he receive any mail. He was, however, considered an able conversationalist who could talk at length on a variety of topics. Dahmer moreover did not outwardly display his anger, or any other emotions for that matter, during his first year in West Germany. Once he started drinking more heavily, however, he began to provoke fights and make negative comments about African Americans and homosexuals.

In early 1981, Dahmer's drinking grew increasingly worse. He became outwardly more racist in his opinions and made racist remarks directly to members of his own unit. He began to miss time at work, and when he did show up he was staggering drunk. His drinking grew so out of control that he could not keep a thought in his head for more than a few seconds. He was soon placed under house arrest. The army wanted to provide Dahmer with some assistance by placing him in an alcohol rehabilitation programme. Eventually they forced him into rehab, but the attempt was unsuccessful, partly because he resisted all assistance and partly because he was so far gone that there was no way to rehabilitate him. Dahmer had all of his freedoms and rights stripped away from him and was found unsuitable for military service due to alcohol dependence. He received a discharge just short of his three-year enlistment and was returned to the United States on 24 March 1981. Two days later, he was formally discharged.

After Dahmer was discharged from the army, his father cut him off almost completely because he was seen as an embarrassment and a total failure. His stepmother kept in touch with him and wanted him desperately to return to Ohio, because she felt that his life was falling apart and that she could help him if he lived closer to her. In October that year, he decided to accept his stepmother's offer and returned to Ohio, where he was arrested on 7 December following an altercation in a bar. Already disappointed in his eldest son, Lionel Dahmer decided that the only person left alive that could discipline Jeffrey was his grandmother, Catherine Dahmer, who welcomed her grandson into her West Allis home with open arms. Dahmer would later tell police that his grandmother was the only person in the world who had ever really loved him.

The move to West Allis seemed to pay off, at least initially. Dahmer quickly obtained a job at a blood bank, working as a phlebotomist. He held the position until he was laid off in 1982. He then began to frequent gay bars and bathhouses on an almost daily basis. On 8 August, at the Wisconsin State Fair Park, he exposed himself to a crowd of women and children. Arrested for disorderly conduct, Dahmer fell into a deep depression and spent both 1983 and 1984 living off the generosity of his aging grandmother. In January 1985, he finally obtained a job at the Ambrosia Chocolate Company, where he worked the night shift. The position provided Dahmer with ample opportunity to experiment with several different homemade sleeping potions at several different bathhouses.

On 8 August 1986 Jeffrey Dahmer was again arrested. This time he was picked up at the Kinnickinnic River for masturbating in public. Seven months later, he received a sentence of a year's probation and counselling for the crime. The murders for which he would become infamous began only four months after this embarrassing sentence.

Dahmer picked up Stephen Thomi in July 1987 and took him to the Ambassador Hotel. He drugged Thomi, murdered him, shoved his body in a suitcase and then brought him to his grandmother's house. There he dismembered the body, ground up the bones and flesh, and disposed of them in the trash.

One year later, Dahmer offered James Doxtator some money to pose for a few pictures, claiming that he was a photographer. The two ended up having sex in the basement of Dahmer's grandmother's house, before Doxtator was drugged and strangled to death. Dahmer dismembered the body and melted it down with a powerful acid solution to clean off the bones, which were then crushed with a sledgehammer, like those of Steven Hicks. Dahmer poured the mixture of flesh and acid down the drain and disposed of the other remains by throwing them in the trash.

Dahmer's grandmother eventually became suspicious of her grandson's activities. Thomi's remains made the house smell horrible, and Dahmer placed the acid solutions which contained James Doxtator's organs in the garage. Catherine Dahmer called her son, Lionel, and told him that he needed to have a talk with Jeffrey. Jeffrey told his father that he was conducting an experiment with some chickens. On 10 March 1988 Dahmer filled out his last report with his probation officer stemming from the incident at the fair. He was discharged from his probation ten days later. On that very same day, Dahmer met Richard Guerrero at the Phoenix Bar. The two had oral sex and Guerrero was drugged. Shortly after, Dahmer's grandmother walked in on the two men having sex and quickly retreated up the stairs. After his grandmother left, Dahmer strangled Guerrero to death. He dismembered him, dissolved the flesh, and disposed of the waste down the drain.

Realising that committing murder was easy, Dahmer established a pattern of looking for victims in the evening hours during the week. On Saturdays he would pick up his victims, and he would dispose of their remains on Sunday morning, while his grandmother was praying for his soul at church. One of the victims who lived to tell police about his encounter with Jeffrey Dahmer was Ernest Flowers, who met Dahmer on 23 April 1988, as he attempted to fix his car. Dahmer offered to give Flowers a ride in a cab so they could pick up Dahmer's car, then return with Flowers to his vehicle and jump start it. Once inside Dahmer's house, Flowers made the nearly fatal mistake of accepting a cup of coffee from the serial killer. Flowers noticed that Dahmer was hiding what he was doing as he made the coffee.

After Dahmer resorted to another means of rendering him unconscious, Ernest Flowers escaped death only because Catherine Dahmer had seen her grandson bring the man home. Disappointed, Dahmer put Flowers in a cab and took him to the local hospital, where he left him. Ernest Flowers woke up the next morning in the hospital and filed a report with the police. Although the police did interview Dahmer regarding the incident, he vehemently denied the allegations and no charges were ever filed against him.

As a result of the botched Ernest Flowers incident, Jeffrey Dahmer was informed by his family that he needed to move out of his grandmother's house. On 25 September 1988, Dahmer moved into his own apartment on North 25th Street. The apartment would soon become Dahmer's own personal killing ground, a safe haven for him to act out the violent fantasies that had completely engulfed him. The day after Dahmer moved into his own place, he approached Sounthome Sinthasomphone about posing for some pictures. Dahmer offered the young man fifty dollars to pose. Sinthasomphone refused to take his clothes off as Dahmer requested, but the serial killer, enraptured in his fantasy of companionship and violence, took the pictures anyway. As part of the ritual, Sinthasomphone was drugged by Dahmer, but the substance did not take immediate effect. Later, Dahmer attempted to grab the young man's penis and started to passionately kiss his bare stomach before allowing him to leave. Sinthasomphone passed out and was taken to hospital, where he told police what had happened to him. Jeffrey Dahmer was arrested for second-degree sexual assault and for enticing a minor for immoral purposes. Convicted of both charges on 30 January 1989, Dahmer was allowed to remain free on bond until it was time for his sentencing hearing in May.

Inadvertently allowed to continue his murderous ways by the oblivious local law enforcement authorities, Jeffrey Dahmer picked up Anthony Sears and Jeffrey Connor at a club called La Cage on 25 March. He was able to convince Sears to accompany him to Dahmer's apartment for drinks; Connor drove them there. Sears was murdered in the same ritualistic fashion as Dahmer's other victims, but this time Dahmer made the crucial decision to preserve his victim's head. He placed the head in a pot of boiling water, then peeled away the layers of skin and spray-painted it grey.

At his sentencing hearing in May 1989, Prosecutor Gale Shelton adamantly tried to convince the court that Dahmer should be sentenced to a minimum of six years on the Sinthasomphone assault because Dahmer was obviously disturbed and was a danger to society. Shelton argued that the sum of Dahmer's activities pointed to a larger pattern of abuse and that he had already been given one chance to change his ways, but had refused to do so. The defence countered that Dahmer's sentence should be based on the effects of sending him to prison, as opposed to the effects of sending him to a rehabilitation or counselling programme. Gerald Boyer argued for the defence that Dahmer was an alcoholic who was extremely sick and desperately needed help, not punishment. He suggested giving Dahmer a suspended sentence, which would go into effect if, and only if, Dahmer received the necessary treatment for his addiction.

The judge was lenient, sentencing Dahmer to five years in prison, which he suspended to five years' probation. He was sentenced to spend a year inside the House of Correction and to undergo another year of psychological treatment. This was for the assault charge.

On the second charge of enticing a minor for immoral purposes, Dahmer was sentenced to three years in prison. The judge, however, stayed his sentence and added an additional five years' probation. Dahmer was also forbidden from having any contact with juveniles. Rather than having Dahmer serve his sentence at the House of Correction, the judge later changed this to the Community Correctional Center. Despite being confined during the day, Dahmer continued to go to work at night and was only fifteen blocks from his apartment.

Jeffrey Dahmer disliked the facility and the large number of minorities incarcerated along with him. He fantasised about killing African Americans, and was assaulted by several black men while at the Center. He broke the rules on a number of occasions, but still received a twelve-hour pass on Thanksgiving. He was not allowed to consume alcohol on pass and was due back by ten o'clock that night; Dahmer finally wandered in at four in the morning and was staggering drunk. On 10 December 1989, Dahmer wrote to the judge about reducing his sentence. In March 1990, he was released as part of an early-release programme. Dahmer spent ten months in jail, but did not participate in any of the court mandated counselling and rehabilitation programmes. Lionel Dahmer pleaded with the court not to release his son until he had completed the court-mandated programmes. His pleas were ignored.

Dahmer's probation officer, Donna Chester, placed strict rules on the probation. She ordered him to meet her twice a month and to undergo a substance abuse treatment programme, and also forbade him from having any unsupervised contact with minors. Dahmer was also expected to attend a psychotherapy programme for his issues with sexuality, and was forbidden from consuming alcohol. By the end of May, Jeffrey Dahmer had returned to the gay bar scene, violating his parole. He met Ricky Beeks at the 219 Club on the 29th and offered him money to be the model for some pictures, but this time the modus operandi differed from Dahmer's previous murders, indicating that his sexual dysfunction, exacerbated by the time he had spent locked up, had moved even further from what might be considered normal. He did not engage in sexual intercourse before drugging Beeks; on this occasion, he incapacitated his victim first. Once Beeks was unconscious, Dahmer strangled him, then performed oral sex with the corpse before dismembering it. He preserved Beeks' skull and painted it.

Dahmer picked up Eddie Smith on 14 June 1990 at the Phoenix Club. He killed and dismembered Smith as he had his previous victims, but did not preserve the skull. This time, Dahmer disposed of the body by placing it out with the trash as he had with the victims murdered inside his grandmother's home. Meeting with his parole officer eleven days after murdering Eddie Smith, Dahmer complained about being depressed. Nearly two weeks later, he picked up a fifteen-year-old Hispanic boy and brought him back to his apartment. The boy posed naked for some pictures, but then wanted to leave. Dahmer panicked and struck the boy on the head with a rubber mallet until he was unconscious, since he had run out of money to buy the ingredients he needed to make the proper sleeping potions. Dahmer attempted to strangle the boy, but the would-be victim fought back. Dahmer calmly explained that he simply did not want the boy to leave because he enjoyed his company, but the boy convinced Dahmer to let him go by promising not to tell anyone about the incident. No charges were ever filed in the attack.

During the two meetings with his probation officer in August 1990, Dahmer continued to complain about being depressed, talking repeatedly about committing suicide and the state of his financial affairs. His probation officer made some suggestions, but he was resistant to most of them. What was regarded as reluctance and lack of co-operation on Dahmer's part was actually a sign that Dahmer had entered the downward spiral associated with serial murder and the fantasy addiction model, in which the acting out of the fantasy never again satisfies the killer because the fantasy has completely taken over every aspect of the killer's life. The depression which Dahmer repeatedly discussed is similar to that a drug addict or alcoholic experiences when he no longer experiences a high, no matter how much of the drug or drink he ingests. At this point in the progression, there is no bringing the addict back to the previously experienced high ever again. Dahmer had reached the stage in his killing spree in which the only way out of the depression was to stop killing, or to become addicted to a new fantasy. He had hit rock bottom. But neither of these options was possible for Dahmer, and he continued to commit murders in the hope that by fulfilling the fantasy that had completely taken hold of him, he would once again reach the psychological high he had previously experienced when committing murder.

On 2 September he met Ernest Miller. Once again Dahmer changed his modus operandi slightly, because Miller was particularly muscular. The two had sex, then Miller was drugged and passed out. Rather than strangle him, Dahmer slashed his carotid artery with a kitchen knife. Miller's body was dismembered and the flesh dissolved in acid. The skull was preserved and later painted. Dahmer also preserved Miller's biceps and placed them in a neat package inside the freezer. He would later cook and consume pieces from them, claiming that it was a way to keep Miller with him forever.

Dahmer saw his parole officer, Donna Chester, eight days after murdering Ernest Miller. Chester chastised Dahmer for not working hard enough on solving his problems, and told him that he had a lot of work to do. A few days later, he picked up David Thomas. He did not have sex with Thomas and claimed later that he had only murdered the young man because he had grown nervous about letting him go after he had drugged him. By the time he was done with Thomas's body, there was nothing left to dispose of.

After a three-month break he started killing again, picking up Curtis Straughter at a bus stop. Straughter was drugged and strangled to death before Dahmer subjected the corpse to oral sex and dismemberment. Once again he preserved the skull. While he was in the process of committing the murder, Dahmer's mother phoned him. The call provided Dahmer with a genuine feeling of warmth that he had not previously experienced, and this opened the door to the primal rage he felt about his youth and the feelings of abandonment that his mother had inflicted upon him. Bothered by the phone call and the emotions he had experienced as a result of it, Dahmer murdered Erol Lindsey on 7 April. He later claimed that the phone call from his mother had had a profound effect on him because he realised that if she had been warm and loving when he was younger, he never would have turned to murder as a means of coping with the reality he was forced to endure. He claimed that he resented his mother for loving him too late, after he had done horrible things that he could never take back and that no one could ever understand.

Dahmer's next murder would anger members of the homosexual community in Milwaukee more than any of his other crimes. On 24 May 1991, Dahmer murdered Anthony Hughes. Hughes was a deaf-mute who had been friends with Dahmer for several years. This was not a safe kill for Dahmer, because he was seen as he left the 219 Club with Hughes and was known to be close friends with him. The murder of Anthony Hughes was probably the first murder that Dahmer committed while fighting against the downward spiral in which he was being swallowed up. There is little doubt that Dahmer murdered Hughes to draw attention to himself, since more conventional appeals for help had failed.

Konerak Sinthasomphone, aged fourteen and the brother of the boy he had drugged in order to take photographs, was picked up by Dahmer on 26 May 1991. Dahmer drugged the boy and performed oral sex on him while he was unconscious. Acting in the downward spiral of his addiction to murder, he made what should have been a crucial mistake in his killing spree, by leaving the young boy alone for several minutes as he went to the store to purchase some beer. While his tormentor was gone, Sinthasomphone made his way to the street, where Nicole Childress spotted him and called 911 to request help for the boy, who was obviously drugged and bleeding. Dahmer arrived home just in time to see Sinthasomphone surrounded by a group of concerned citizens. Then the police arrived. Dahmer grabbed the boy, but was stopped by the authorities. Explaining that the boy was his lover and that they had had a fight, Dahmer was able to convince the police to return with him and the boy to his apartment, where he would explain the situation in greater detail. Sinthasomphone could not tell his side of the story because of the drugs he had been given. Police accompanied Dahmer back to his apartment, but did not search the premises despite the foul stench which emanated from the domicile. They left Sinthasomphone with Dahmer and radioed to dispatch, saying, 'Intoxicated Asian, naked male. Was returned to his sober boyfriend.' On the police tapes, the officers could be heard laughing.

Once they were alone, Dahmer strangled his latest victim, had oral sex with him, and then dismembered the body. The corpse of Anthony Hughes was still in the bedroom, so Dahmer placed Sinthasomphone's head in the freezer and his torso into the 57-gallon drum of acid he kept inside the apartment. The next day, Dahmer met his probation officer. The story of the murder of Konerak Sinthasomphone would later outrage the entire city of Milwaukee. The police officers who had responded to the call received suspensions, but the damage had already been done to the relationship between the citizens of Milwaukee and those who were sworn to protect them.

By this time, Dahmer's alcoholism had grown worse than ever before. His grandmother had become ill and he was almost out of money. Further complications soon followed. Since he had missed so many days of work, he was in danger of losing his job. Dahmer could no longer break free of the cycle of drinking and killing which fed his hatred and rage. He had two serious addictions which he was battling against: one to commit murder and the other to consume alcohol. Although the alcohol addiction had, to some degree, contributed to his killing spree by lowering his inhibitions, it also stood alone as a powerful and detrimental force in his life. The interplay between these two addictions is interesting in the study of serial murder, as other serial killers have also utilised the numbing effects of alcohol to help them commit their crimes; but Dahmer's addiction to alcohol was particularly problematic even notwithstanding its effect on his urge to kill. In the end, the battle between the two addictions had festered inside Dahmer's troubled mind for so long that each destroyed the other, in turn destroying any shred of humanity to which he had been clinging. The more he drank, the easier it was to commit murder; but the more he drank, the more depressed he became. This fuelled his need to kill in a never-ending cataclysmic cycle of destruction, which allowed him no solace and no release from anything or anyone.

In June 1991, Jeffrey Dahmer met Brother John Paul Ranier, who ran a street ministry for homosexuals in the Milwaukee area. Ranier would later say that he never saw Dahmer sober. Dahmer told Ranier about his hatred of blacks and homosexuals and went against his previous acceptance of his own homosexuality by stating that he was not gay. Completely denying who he was, Dahmer told Ranier that he was a straight man who was unable to have a relationship with a woman. He claimed that he wanted to be with a woman, but was frustrated and overwhelmed in the presence of females. Dahmer made bold statements that were completely unfounded. He told Ranier that homosexuals were responsible for AIDS, and claimed that his father too hated homosexuals.

The conversations that Dahmer had with Ranier provide insights into the way in which his mind was working towards the end of his murderous rampage. The feelings he had about his mother not loving him and her subsequent abandonment of him were probably the key contributors to his feelings of awkwardness around women. In his mind, he believed that if his own mother could not love him, he must not be worthy of such love, and therefore that no other woman would love him either. After having accepted his sexual orientation as a youth of eighteen, Dahmer's statements regarding hatred for homosexuals during his killing spree are examples of the self-hatred that he felt. He did not hate homosexuals for their sexual orientation, but because they reminded him that he was different from mainstream society. This difference, compounded by the fact that he already felt abandoned by the world, only fuelled the hatred he had for himself. By stating that his father also hated homosexuals, Dahmer was achieving one of two things. Either he was searching for a common ground that he and his father could share, since his father had disowned and was ashamed of him, or he was stating his conviction that his father hated him because he was a homosexual, without making this sense explicit. In either case, these statements reveal a great deal about the confusion running amok inside his head during his last few days as a free man and serial killer.

Further tempting the police, who on at least three occasions failed to lock Jeffrey Dahmer up before he continued to kill any more innocent people, Dahmer violated his parole a number of times by taking frequent bus trips to Chicago on weekends. On one visit, he met a man named Matt Turner and convinced him to return with Dahmer to Milwaukee to have some pictures taken. After taking the Greyhound bus, the two caught a cab to Dahmer's apartment, where Turner was murdered and disposed of. Turner's head was placed in the freezer, and his torso in the drum of acid. Days later, Dahmer returned to Chicago and met Jeremiah Weinberger, who he also brought home to Milwaukee. Weinberger met the same grisly fate as Turner.

Nine days later, Dahmer was fired from his job at the chocolate factory because of excessive absences and tardiness. The next day, he met and murdered Oliver Lacy. Joseph Bradehoft, married with three children, had the misfortune to meet Jeffrey Dahmer on 19 July, soon after Dahmer had left a meeting with his parole officer. The two men had oral sex before Bradehoft was drugged, strangled and dismembered. His head was placed beside Oliver Lacy's inside Dahmer's freezer. Joseph Bradehoft was to be Jeffrey Dahmer's final victim.

On 22 July 1991, Milwaukee policemen Robert Rauth and Rolf Mueller saw Tracy Edwards running down a street at 11.30 p.m. Edwards had a pair of handcuffs dangling from his left wrist. The police began to question him about the handcuffs. Edwards told them about the four hours of torture he had suffered at the hands of Jeffrey Dahmer. According to Edwards, Dahmer had invited him back to his apartment for drinks, and then handcuffs were placed on him at knifepoint. Dahmer threatened to eat Edwards' heart while they watched *The Exorcist III*. When he saw his opportunity, Edwards escaped from the apartment.

Dahmer had claimed that he was a photographer and wanted to take some pictures of Edwards, for which he would be paid. The pictures were to be of a nude Tracy Edwards. Edwards was with two other gentlemen when Dahmer approached them. He agreed to accompany Dahmer to his apartment on North 25th Street, while his two companions would return home to meet up later with Edwards at Dahmer's apartment for drinks. Dahmer had intentionally given Edwards' companions the wrong address, and prepared to carry out the same plan he had used successfully with so many others in the past. Apparently Edwards felt comfortable with Dahmer, because he was not concerned when the cab that the two men took to the apartment stopped a block away from where Dahmer had said that it was supposed to be. Edwards did not become nervous, even when he entered the apartment and was suddenly overwhelmed by a horrible stench, because the rest of the apartment appeared to him to be quite normal. Edwards accepted Dahmer's explanation about the odour, which was that the sewer pipes behind the walls had burst and the smell was emanating from them. To explain the boxes of acid in his apartment, Dahmer told Edwards that he did not have anywhere else to store the chemicals, which he used to clean bricks.

Dahmer attempted to subdue Edwards with a concoction of alcohol mixed with drugs. Once his victim was unconscious, Dahmer would handcuff, strip and rape him. After the rape, he would murder and dismember him while taking Polaroid photos of every step of the act. Edwards was not a big drinker, however, so the plan did not work the way that Dahmer had expected. It was when Edwards approached the aquarium inside Dahmer's apartment that the serial killer, completely destroyed by his fantasies, pulled a knife on him and placed the handcuffs on his wrists. Edwards explained that Dahmer's face and body changed as if they had undergone a physical transformation. One moment Dahmer became aggressive and his muscles tightened up, while the next he relaxed and became gentle with his victim.

Edwards also reported that it was during the demonic sections of *The Exorcist III* that Dahmer became most aggressive. It was as though the demons in the movie had possessed Dahmer. Edwards began to carefully study Dahmer's behaviour and noted the times he lost the aggressive urges and became totally engrossed in the movie, times during which he did not pay attention to Edwards. Edwards also noted that when he talked to Dahmer during his aggressor's most violent periods, Dahmer calmed down. Edwards had discovered an important truth about serial killers: in order to calm them down, you must allow them to express their feelings and fantasies. Any attempt on the part of a victim to open the door to communication with a killer is likely to be successful, at least temporarily.

As the night wore on, Dahmer grew to trust Edwards, allowing him to leave the bedroom and sit in the living room, where the air conditioning was a reprieve from the bedroom's stifling air. Once inside the living room, Edwards requested permission to go to the rest-room. Dahmer allowed him to go, almost without paying attention to him. This was the crucial mistake that Dahmer was compelled to make, as he had reached the end of the line. Murder no longer satisfied his fantasies, and at the subconscious level Dahmer wished to be apprehended so that he could confess his crimes and relive them in the public eye. Tracy Edwards, seizing the opportunity, slammed into Dahmer, knocking him off balance. He then ran for the front door.

The police accompanied Tracy Edwards back to Jeffrey Dahmer's apartment, 213 North 25th Street. The serial killer was not surprised. The results of this inquiry would be completely different from the time police returned Konerak Sinthasomphone back to the apartment a few months earlier. This time, police ran a check for prior arrests and warrants on Dahmer. They discovered that Dahmer had a pair of felony convictions for sexual assault and was currently on probation. Dahmer, in a primal release of years of penned up anger and loneliness, let out a terrible scream before surrendering and being placed in custody. The serial killer and cannibal was finally at peace, no longer haunted by the demons that had turned him into a fantasy-addicted monster.

Inside the apartment, police discovered a mess in the kitchen, power tools in the living room, and bloodstains on the bed. Dozens of Polaroid photographs were strewn about the apartment. The pictures were of bloodied corpses in various stages of dissection. There were also photos of severed human remains, which Dahmer kept as souvenirs. One particular photograph depicted a severed head which had been painted gold and placed on top of a pair of severed hands. In the refrigerator, police located the skull of one of Dahmer's victims in a box on the shelf. In the freezer there was a human heart, and in a separate freezer which sat on the floor there were three additional human heads. The bedroom contained a box full of pictures and two additional skulls. Three more skulls, along with several human bones, were found inside a filing cabinet. Inside the closet, there were two skulls in a kettle, and in a second pot were found assorted male genitalia and several severed hands. Police also located the 57-gallon drum Dahmer kept in the bedroom, which was filled with acid and three headless torsos.

As part of his fantasy, Dahmer obtained a sexual thrill from taking pictures of the posed corpses. He also derived sexual pleasure from dehumanising his victims. This allowed him to become superior to them, and also shows the way that he felt about himself because of inner feelings of abandonment and isolation. In his detailed fantasies, Dahmer was precise and methodical in his technique for dismembering the corpses of his victims. By paying attention to detail, he could devise ways to wear certain parts of his victims, much like another infamous Wisconsin serial murderer, Ed Gein. Gein became the model for both the main character in the film *Psycho* and the character of Buffalo Bill in *The Silence of the Lambs*. Dahmer could also reassemble the body parts in any way he pleased, which gave him a sense of total power and control. These were feelings which he could not experience without committing murder.

Dahmer was capable of living inside the apartment with such a horrible odour because he had become desensitised to all smells. Most serial killers have sensory impairments because their olfactory nerves are damaged or because they suffer from a neurological disorder that emerges from damage to the brain caused by toxins in the environment. In Dahmer's case, his addiction to alcohol contributed to the repression of the normal functioning of his neurological systems.

Jeffrey Dahmer motivated himself to continue to live from one murder to the next by rearranging the body parts of his victims. By handling the different parts and having masturbatory sex over them, he was empowered and felt like he had finally gained control over his life. As part of his fantasy of permanent companionship this is quite significant, because as long as he owned the body parts, no one could ever truly leave him. This was by far the most enticing part of the fantasy to Dahmer. Another significant act relating to his hopes of fulfilling his fantasy of permanent companionship was his attempt to completely own his victims and to incorporate them into his own body by consuming their vital organs. He utilised cannibalism like no other serial killer before him, to refortify the iron and vitamins in his system, which had been depleted by his chronic abuse of alcohol.

Investigators began to question Dahmer's neighbours after his arrest. Gene Mitchell, the building manager of the structure adjacent to Dahmer's, said that he could smell the foul odour of decaying flesh throughout the entire neighbourhood. The manager of Dahmer's own building, Larry Marion, agreed, and added that an elderly neighbour who lived above Dahmer had become deathly ill because of the stench and had been forced to move. Both men, however, had believed that the odour was caused by a sewage back-up or leakage. Other neighbours reported that they had been able to hear the sounds of saws coming from the apartment at all hours of the day.

Jeffrey Dahmer was ready to confess his crimes almost immediately after he was placed in custody. The rush of freedom that he experienced on being apprehended led him to want a clean soul, and the only way to become completely free of the horrors which had fuelled his bloody and macabre murder spree was to confess totally to every grisly detail. Dahmer admitted to being on parole at the time of his arrest for the sexual assault of a minor, then began to talk about the murders, beginning with that of Steven Hicks. In total, Dahmer confessed to eleven brutal murders on the day of his arrest. He told police that the only difficulty he had found with killing was that the disposal of the bodies took too much time. Another problem he had encountered was that with all the murders he committed, he did not have sufficient room to store the remains of his victims. To solve the problem, he had purchased the 57-gallon drum and filled it with acid.

Dahmer continued to be an open book about his crimes, until police mentioned cannibalism. The very realisation and admission that he had eaten the flesh of his victims was too much for Dahmer to bear, so he stopped talking. His final comments were about masturbating in front of his victims' body parts. Dahmer and his attorney, Gerald Boyle, decided that he would claim that at the time of his crimes he had suffered from a mental illness and was incapable of telling the difference between right and wrong, under Wisconsin state law. The mental illness they would specify was necrophilia.

Prosecutor Michael McCann stated that Dahmer's murders, dismemberments and sexual activity with the corpses did not point to a mental illness. He argued that Dahmer did know right from wrong because he concealed what he was doing from the public by using the drum of acid as a method to dispose of his victims. McCann also pointed out that Dahmer's crimes were premeditated, because he had been very selective in his choice of victims and because he had prepared his sedative powders in advance of the crimes.

Jeffrey Dahmer did premeditate his crimes, which were spurred on by an unhealthy addiction to perverse sexual fantasies about coerced companionship. Although most organised serial killers disguise what they have done from the public and conceal the bodies of their victims, Jeffrey Dahmer did not conceal or dispose of them on account of his knowledge that what he was doing was wrong. Unlike most serial killers who dispose of victims and conceal their bodies to avoid apprehension and as an afterthought to the fantasy, he instead incorporated the disposal of his victims into the fantasy itself.

The disposal of victims had to be an inclusive part of Dahmer's fantasy because the fantasy involved total possession of his victims and permanent companionship. Rather than dispose of his victims for the sake of getting rid of evidence, Dahmer eliminated only the parts he no longer needed. Polaroid photos of the dismembered corpses littered the apartment in which he lived. His refrigerator contained only condiments and beer, along with human body parts. There was a stench emanating from the apartment that several people noticed. If anyone had taken the time to investigate the smell or the sounds of sawing during the day, they would have walked right into Dahmer's own private hell. He derived pleasure from spending time with the dead bodies and mutilated remains, and had attempted to create zombies out of several of his victims. Once the endeavour had proved unsuccessful and his victims had perished, Dahmer had no choice but to keep them. He was compelled to keep them hidden because his fantasy life did not allow for him to share what he believed was truly his. If he had simply disposed of the victims by the roadside, such as the Hillside Stranglers had done, he would not have remained true to the very fantasy which had sustained his life and to which he had become addicted. There was no deception on Dahmer's part in his disposing of his victims. It was part of his fantasy and, as such, lent credence to the supposition that he did not recognise that what he was doing was wrong.

Even if Jeffrey Dahmer could have understood that what he was doing was wrong, he suffered from a sexual disease and was incapable of conforming his behaviour to the law. The necrophilia rendered him incapable of making appropriate decisions with regard to his actions. He was not in control of himself, but was rather controlled by his disease and by the addiction to his fantasies, as well as his addiction to alcohol. For these reasons he should have been found insane, the defence argued. Dr Frank Berlin of Johns Hopkins University testified that Dahmer suffered from necrophilia. He argued that Dahmer was compelled to kill because the only way that he could have sex was with a dead person. Therefore, even if Dahmer knew that killing was wrong, he could not conform his behaviour to the law, due to this compulsion. Dr Judith Becker of the University of Arizona concurred with Dr Berlin's testimony. Becker stated that Dahmer had admitted to performing lobotomies on his victims in order to turn them into zombies who would never be able to abandon him. She also described Dahmer's temple fantasy, in which an altar would be built utilising the body parts of his victims. She argued that he had no sense of self, and that he believed that he actually possessed magical powers. The pleasure that he obtained from the dead bodies made him believe that he had even greater powers, Becker argued.

On 1 May 1992, after just six hours of deliberation, the jury found Jeffrey Dahmer guilty of sixteen counts of murder and he was sentenced to sixteen life sentences. He was murdered in jail by another inmate, while working as a janitor within the general prison population.

Jeffrey Dahmer had always been a loner. He reacted out of the anger he felt over his repressed homosexual desires, and his acting out, in the form of serial murder, was a display of dominance. He acted in complete opposition to any normal sexual intercourse. He had been excluded from his own family, and whatever the true situation, Dahmer felt that he was the forgotten and least favourite child. He constantly exhibited hostility towards his mother and younger brother. From this hostility, Dahmer quickly learned that he could deal with these feelings best by asserting control over something that could not prevent him from doing so, such as a small animal – or, later in life, a drugged and incapacitated victim. The more satisfaction he obtained from this belief, the more control he sought, and the deeper his addiction to the fantasy became. Dahmer never established traditional boundaries between himself and others, because of his fantasy addiction. He never developed a genuine sense of self or a personality. As a result, he attempted to discover exactly how much he could destroy and still get away with it. This also developed into a fascination with the independence of others and how he could take it away from them, so that they would never be able to abandon him the way his family had done.

Dahmer, initially accepting of his homosexuality, eventually became overwrought with shame about both his sexuality and his first murder. These feelings invaded all aspects of his life and literally controlled him from the day he murdered Steven Hicks until the day Tracy Edwards escaped his clutches. When he moved into his own apartment and away from the watchful eye of his grandmother, he guaranteed himself privacy. It was a place where his fantasies could become realities without anyone ever knowing about them. One of the main ingredients of Dahmer's fantasy was privacy. He wanted to be alone with his companions, who would later become his victims. This explains why he never committed any murders while he was in the army or attending Ohio State University.

Jeffrey Dahmer physically and emotionally continued to run away from his crimes by distancing himself from what he had done. At the same time, he was forced to deal with the intense feelings of sexual gratification he obtained from the commission of these crimes. Therefore, the part of Dahmer which should have been positive and productive was overpowered by a desperate need for privacy and a companion to gratify his needs. Because of this, he destroyed what seemed to be a successful military and college career in order to commit murder. Additionally, his addiction to alcohol rendered him a slave to his need to consume liquor, which was done, in part, to lower his inhibitions while murdering his victims. In this vicious circle of dual addiction, Dahmer drowned.

In Dahmer's case, listening to the life inside a person or feeling the pulse of blood as it moved through someone's body was the only act of bonding he had ever been capable of exhibiting. The latter was an act that nearly always occurred during or near sexual intercourse. It was the safest way for Dahmer to show that he loved someone.

Dahmer is different from other serial killers for several reasons. First, he came from an upper middle class, apparently normal family. He lived with family members during the commission of at least some of his crimes, and he kept in contact with his family during the commission of his murders. His fear of being abandoned gave rise to his fantasies, and also to a pathological desire to control other people. By controlling them, he was controlling his own fears. This feeling did not last, so he had to commit additional murders. By the end of it all, even murder did not allow him to control his fears, and he allowed Tracy Edwards to escape so that he could finally be free for once in his life. Incapable of socialising or interacting with other living people in a normal way, Dahmer was constantly preoccupied with his fantasies and his own need for survival, which was sustained through turning the fantasies into reality. The primitive components of Jeffrey Dahmer's nervous system, and particularly his pleasure/pain centres within the temporal lobe, were the most vital functions of his behaviour. He was empty inside, and by dismembering his victims he could recall the pleasurable feelings he had experienced in his youth, when he dismembered small animals. These were moments of bonding for Dahmer, and he could not let his victims survive; but nor could he get rid of them completely, because to do so would leave him in agony. For this reason, he preserved their body parts much as he had done with his animals.

While Dahmer was clearly a necrophiliac, he was also a paraphiliac, which means he was sexually stimulated by objects which are generally considered not to be sexual in nature. Jeffrey Dahmer committed a truly heinous series of murders, but if there is anyone in the history of true crime who was insane and did not know right from wrong, he is that person.

8. THE MEDICAL MODEL

To properly understand the enormity that the problem of serial murder poses for society at large, one need only examine the crimes of serial killers such as Arthur Shawcross, Eugene Britt and Hadden Clark, and multiply these atrocities by five hundred. Add to this the crimes of Douglas Clark and Randy Kraft, as well as the thousands of others not profiled in this work, and the scope of the problem presents itself as it is – endless. Although these and other atrocious crimes dominate the headlines of print media, as well as taking up a significant amount of time in television and radio news programmes, the situation is not hopeless. While it is true that the problem of serial murder is spreading, advances in the study of this phenomenon continue to bring success in the apprehension of these individuals. According to a 1988 FBI report, there are at least 35 serial killers on the loose at any given moment, and this estimate does not include the number of unsolved homicide cases around the world that continue to confound investigators. The hope lies, in some part, in recent discoveries and acknowledgements made on behalf of medical and law enforcement personnel regarding a medical model of serial murder.

Since the inception of the term 'serial killer' in the 1970s, over seven thousand people have fallen victim to this type of murderer, with the number growing steadily every year. Once professionals made the bold choice to understand how episodic killers are shaped by such patterned events as child abuse, poor parenting, brain injuries, neurological disorders, cognitive disorders, malnutrition, drug and alcohol abuse, and poisoning from various other toxins in the natural environment, the true nature of the serial killer became a little clearer. These discoveries have led to new approaches for the study of this type of violent offender.

The serial killer is wholly unlike any other form of violent criminal and as such he must be studied and examined using a multiplicity of methods. This type of study often requires means that are unconventional, untested, and outright radical. The medical model of serial murder is one such method of study, as are the other models profiled in this book. While the acceptance of this or any other model posited in this work may be difficult to swallow for several reasons, we must not be blinded by our past failings when dealing with the serial murderer. It is certainly easier to demonise such an individual in the press and in our minds, rather than to recognise that the serial killer is a human being, like the rest of us, who has acted out of some diagnosable disease. But as research into the field expands and is taken more seriously by other disciplines, this realisation is becoming more and more of a viable possibility.

Professionals in the fields of sociology, psychology and criminology have taken great strides in their efforts to understand the functions and mechanisms of violent criminal behaviour. One revelation relevant to the medical model is that cycles of violence, regardless of what form they take, have been initiated through previous generations, and follow a process by which each successive generation feeds upon the dysfunctions of the preceding ones. A negative environment in sustained by this process. Violence, in any form, is a learned behaviour. As its teachings are reinforced and compounded by outside influences, such as the media and the entertainment industry, a *society* of violence and apathy steadily emerges. The concentric society, which becomes numb to violence, provides a sustainable environment in which violence can thrive.

The medical model is a significant and viable platform from which to approach the study of serial murder, as it links the types of violence exhibited in these crimes to various patterns of abuse. Patterns of psychological abuse, compounded by neurological disease and pervasive self-destructive behaviours, are present in the lives and psyches of a vast number of known serial killers. As with other diseases, there is a pool of diagnosable symptoms that sufferers will exhibit. Not every person exhibits all the symptoms within the pool, but they will characteristically exhibit enough of the symptoms to be linked to others who are afflicted by the same disease. The same holds true for the serial killer within the construct of the medical model. For example, not all serial killers are abused as children, nor are they all drug addicts or alcoholics. They may or may not have a neurological disorder, but they all share enough of the same symptoms to be linked to one another. Consequently, the pool of symptoms constitutes a diagnosable disease with which they can all be attributed in some form.

Traditionally, the serial killer has been labelled and regarded as being either sociopathic or psychotic. While this diagnosis seems suitable to most observers, it does not take into consideration an important element of the serial killer. The medical model takes a critical look at the idea that these individuals lack a traditional personality and are outside the range of normal human existence. This idea postulates that their only problem is that in some way they are deviant and it is this that separates them from the rest of the human race. But this is false, because the serial killer does not fit into the usual realm of human existence and to label him as deviant does not do him justice, and nor does it allow for a treatment plan which may offer some form of effective intervention that could bring him closer to rejoining the human race.

Careful study of a large range of serial killers, such as has been attempted by the FBI and a number of individual researchers, has pointed to evidence that each individual killer displays a set of behaviours or symptoms that have shaped his behaviour in the same way that a cancer patient's appearance and level of functioning is shaped by the set of symptoms from which he or she suffers. During the commission of their crimes, all serial killers sever themselves from whatever sense of reality they are clinging to. They are unable to make the distinction between right and wrong because for them there is no such thing as right and wrong; their only concern is with what is going to satisfy their fantasy. Some serial killers have certainly been known to bury their victims or to conceal their bodies in some way, and this has been misunderstood as a form of sympathy, compassion, or remorse, but it is actually a further symptom of the disease of serial murder.

During the commission of a murder, the serial killer has surrendered his free will to his fantasy and is in the throes of an episodic period of aggression, which can best be described by the term 'frenzy'. Because of this, he does not fit into any of the neat and tidy compartmentalisations which the legal system has created so that it can sort criminals into separate groups. They are beyond even the realm of the traditional definition of insanity and must be dealt with as such. While it is easier, and indeed more appealing, to claim that a serial killer is a monster who has made the conscious choice to act in a particular manner, thereby choosing to ignore the human components of his personality, this ignores the fact that the serial killer is a different creature all to himself. He does not have the capacity for remorse, compassion, proper decision-making, or any other normal human interaction.

Devoid of a personality and a recognisable internal structure to his own life, the serial killer differs from other human beings in that he transforms himself into whatever it will take for him to fit in to the social system he is confronted with. He uses his surroundings to construct an external skeleton upon which to hang his life. This gives the impression that he is in fact capable of controlling his primal urges, as well as deceiving others into believing that he does have a personality and can therefore control aspects of it like the rest of the population. His disease, particularly this aspect of it, explains why most serial killers make model inmates and why it falsely appears that they have improved or made the conscious choice to change their behaviour. Without the external stimuli which helped to prompt the serial killer to murder, and with the addition of a structured environment, medication, and better nutrition, the serial killer hangs his life on a better skeleton, thus tailoring it to what is expected and what is demanded of him. Outside the walls of a prison or other institution that operates on rigidity and strict guidelines for behaviour and conduct, he is overwhelmed by freedom and hangs his life on the skeleton that best suits his fantasy. This is the skeleton that leads him to commit horrific crimes against innocent people. Unchecked by the sort of monitoring and structure found in the penal and institutional systems, the disease that afflicts the serial killer is allowed to run rampant with dire consequences for the rest of the world.

Serial killers are totally reliant upon their external environment for all their sentient activity. The similarities in modus operandi, primal behaviours, results of biochemical tests, and the ways in which serial killers react and adjust to being incarcerated, all point to the fact that serial murder is a disease.

Root causes include genetic defects, brain damage and chemical imbalances, while other symptoms include the absence of self and a hair-trigger violent response to any external stimulus that proves too challenging. Serial killers do not possess the capacity for gauging an appropriate way to react to a stressful or confrontational situation. They react to any challenge with extreme force. Without the ability to determine proportionate violence, the serial killer is at a serious deficit when making decisions of any type. Decision-making in itself is a stressful task, regardless of how trivial the decision may be. They moreover do not perceive punishment as a deterrent to their crimes. Many of them welcome incarceration because of the realisation that they are different and would like to stop killing, but can't without some sort of intervention from an external source.

The psychophysiological mechanisms that prevent most people from acting on their impulses without forethought are absent within the serial killer. To hide this from people he comes into contact with, the serial killer constructs a mask of sanity behind which he hides. This mask allows him to appear normal and carry on some sort of day-to-day functioning within the world. Eugene Britt once described walking a woman home from his neighbour's house, saying, 'She was talking her head off and didn't even know she was walking with a madman.' This mask of sanity is based on what the serial killer gleans from watching normal people behave, but it is shattered when an impulse compels him to act or he finds himself in an overly stressful situation. This mask of sanity serves as a key symptom of the disease of serial murder. It also allows him to lure victims into his trap and serves as a tool he can use to prevent his apprehension.

The serial murderer is different from other types of killer because of his lack of rational behaviour and lack of ability to appreciate the consequences of his actions. This episodic aggression can be characterised by a pattern of root causes including emotional and physical abuse, sexual abuse and other significant trauma, which may be treatable to some extent. If caught early enough in childhood, the patterns may be treated with counselling or other conventional interventions, and could put would-be serial killers on a different path. Indeed, we will never know just how many people have been steered from this path with the appropriate level of life-saving early intervention. Prevention is possible. Unfortunately, the appropriate level of service is not available to everyone; and when there is availability, it is seldom distributed in an equitable manner.

Within the early developmental stages of life, a serial killer demonstrates signs of excessive pathological and grandiose behaviour. The sufferings of a serial killer are internal and often remain a mystery to investigators, even after his apprehension, unless he shares them with his captors. The pattern of suffering, however, occurs at a young age and is expressed in abnormal behaviours, which are often ignored or attributed to other causes and left untreated. If these symptoms go untreated and undiagnosed, the potential serial killer grows to maturity objectifying others and constructing an elaborate and carefully designed fantasy, which becomes a sort of architectural plan for his future violence.

A history of head trauma, or brain and neurological disorders, coupled with psychomotor epilepsy in its various forms, are medical characteristics of serial murder that are just beginning to come to light in areas of serious research. Genetics plays a role because certain forms of epilepsy and other neurological disorders are passed down through generations across the genetic code. Such physiological impairments have a directly negative effect towards both an individual's behaviour and the social controls the individual has at his disposal for controlling and monitoring such behaviour. The existence of a genetic code that predisposes some families to violent behaviour may be easy enough to identify. Consider the pattern of homicide that was present in the family of serial killer Gerald Gallego. His father was on death row for murder, as were his uncle and cousin. And consider the murder sprees of Ralph and Tommy Searl, a pair of brothers who each committed a series of unrelated murders for apparently different reasons. While it is true that not everyone who suffers from a brain injury or other neurological impairment becomes a serial killer, when such injuries are inflicted by abuse or when such problems emerge in a household which is unstable, or when it is fuelled by alcohol and drug abuse and enhanced by malnutrition, the probability that a serial killer may emerge increases dramatically. It is important to keep in mind a fact which is often ignored – the fact that there is no one single factor to which the emergence of a serial killer can be attributed. The same can be said about any other known disease. It is a constellation of the aforementioned factors that creates such an individual.

Because of their disease, serial killers have no external behavioural reference points. Therefore, the reference points which most individuals take for granted must come for the serial killer from within. This leads to the absence of a personality map within the serial killer and is the beginning of the end, for he can no longer control his impulses and negative behaviours.

Malnutrition is an important root cause of serial murder because it can occur both in homes that are stable and unstable, although the known serial killers who have emerged from unstable homes are more likely to exhibit signs of malnutrition. A diet that is weak and deficient in vital vitamins and nutrients deprives the brain of the fuel that it needs to function properly, and also leads to other disorders related to these deficiencies. Iron deficiencies are known to rob the body of its resilience. Zinc and potassium deficiencies lead to hormonal and chemical imbalances that promote a constant state of emotional turmoil. When a body does not receive the proper amounts of vitamins B or C, it is less likely to be able to fight off infection. Many of these infections lead to other medical problems for the serial killer. In killers who suffer from these symptoms, we see outside stimuli met by a knee-jerk reaction that often becomes excessively aggressive and violent.

Substance abuse inhibits the brain from functioning at its optimal capacity. All known serial killers have, at one point or another, experienced the effects of massive quantities of alcohol or drugs. The euphoric state associated with drugs and alcohol is a feeling the serial killer craves, as he is unable to experience happiness otherwise, except when he is committing crimes. This is why many serial killers are drug addicts or alcoholics. Drugs and alcohol also contribute to the serial killer's hallucinatory state and further separate him from consensual reality.

While the brain is at the centre of all life, there is nothing magical about it or the way in which it functions. Consciousness is nothing more than the overlapping of electrochemical messages between the different senses and areas such as recognition, memory and nerves. The brain is a highly sophisticated parallel processor and a subordinating processor. Although this mechanistic model of the brain oversimplifies the tasks that this organ performs, it does not diminish the fact that the brain in its complexity is in charge of a massive electrical-neurological system that controls everything we do.

Most individuals, even if they don't remember their dreams, dream almost every night. The serial killer exists in a semi-dream/semi-waking state, which is episodic in nature and points to a dysfunction within the limbic system. This is dangerous, considering that the limbic system controls our fight or flight reactions. It is also the centre of the brain that reflexively responds to a perceived threat, whether legitimately or not. An exaggerated startle response can trigger a person's impulse to react with excessive violent force. Aspects of the serial killer's dreams intrude upon his waking reality without warning, and this leaves the killer in a state where he is trapped and alone with the terrifying nightmares that haunt him. He is unable, as a result of this condition, to determine whether or not he is asleep or awake. There is no separation or difference between dreams and reality for the serial killer. As a result of this, the serial killer is plagued by a delusional state in which he confuses people and situations from his past. This becomes increasingly dangerous when he eliminates the identities of his victims, reducing them to whatever his troubled mind imposes upon them.

The brain has a gyroscopic capacity to compensate for errors and damage, but it is also this capacity that creates the formula from which serial killers emerge. It is this defence mechanism that turns the individual into a violent predator in its efforts to right what it recognises as wrong. Self-defence is a manifestation of the basic human need to survive. The same emotions that exist in a serial killer for purposes of self-defence, such as fear, rage and terror, also exist in the rest of the population. The serial killer, however, because of his developmental, emotional, neurological and other problems, has to compensate for these anxieties in order to regain the internal balance that the rest of society maintains. In this way, as an extension of the medical model, the serial killer is a psychophysiological mutant, whose internal defence mechanisms have turned against him.

Serial murder is also a disease which results from a series of ongoing organic malfunctions within the individual. It is well known that damage to the temporal lobe, no matter how slight, has been directly linked to violent reactions, as well as to poor impulse control. Serial killers also share a common trait which is directly medical, that of epileptic seizures. Repeated seizures, which are violent in nature, contribute to the negative perception that many serial killers have of themselves. This explains why they are constantly obsessed with thoughts of suicide. Additionally, epileptic seizures contribute heavily to dangerous behaviours that involve an increased level of unacceptable risk.

Electroencephalogram (EEG) testing has proved vital, not only to the study of serial killers as a group but also as a valid scientific support for the medical model of serial murder. It has been demonstrated through extensive testing of individuals who exhibit episodic violence and also suffer from epilepsy that they display sharp vertical spikes on EEG scans, interrupting normal brainwave patterns. Such spikes are indicative of dramatically powerful discharges of very high voltage coursing through the limbic portion of the brain. Electrical discharges, such as the ones revealed by EEG tests, are known to cause damage to the limbic portion of the brain. This is significant considering that it is this portion of the brain that controls both terror and aggression. The brain, as a fragile and highly sensitive organ, can only withstand so many of these electrical discharges before it is completely destroyed and can no longer function as it was designed to do.

Most individuals perform at least a small part of their daily activities according to a stimulus-response model. In the serial murderer, this sort of model assumes a different function. The serial killer's hypothalamus maintains control over the emotional centres of the brain as the killer develops from child to adult. A malfunction of this regulatory mechanism contributes heavily to the appearance of severe mood swings within the killer. Much as a broken thermostat can no longer regulate household temperature, a damaged hypothalamus has a difficult time regulating somatic conditions such as body temperature, appetite and control of emotions. The sufferer becomes unable to control or curb his emotions.

Though serial killers appear to be normal and can demonstrate normal social interaction, some if not most of the time their brains do not function in any way, shape or form as normal brains. All serial killers have been deprived of something in their early development, whether it be nutrition, love, guidance or something else. This deprivation has caused the recognition of boundaries between self and world that occur in normal people never to develop properly. Serial killers are completely unable to recognise the obvious distinction between self and others, as well as reality and fantasy. They are preoccupied to a great extent with themselves and their own needs. As such, they are constantly searching for ways to meet their selfish needs. This leads them to be narcissistic and egotistical. The serial killer believes that there are no limits to what he can do, or what he is allowed to do. He acts without remorse or guilt. These are emotions he has never been shown or taught. Because he cannot empathise with others, he does not recognise them as human beings who think, feel and breathe as he does. This enables him to carry out his twisted fantasies of sex and violence without so much as a second thought.

The most common mistake that is made when dealing with serial killers is that most people are unfamiliar with the complexities of the serial killers' mindsets and falsely believe that these individuals can control their anger, but make the choice not to do so. The fact is that the type of anger experienced by the serial killer cannot be controlled. It is an extension of who he is and cannot be separated from his mental make-up, any more readily than his skin can be removed from his skeleton if he is to survive.

Psychiatrist Kurt Goldstein developed the theory of personality known as Organismic Theory. It is this theory which best details the type of characteristics that a serial killer possesses, while still asserting that he does not possess a personality. This theory postulates that an organism consists of differentiated members which are articulated together. These members do not detach from one another, except under abnormal conditions such as brain injury or excessive stress and anxiety. It is a pivotal consideration for any proper examination of the medical model of serial murder.

Organismic functioning is primarily organised into figures and grounds. Figures are processes that emerge against a particular background, and occupy the centre of attentiveness. Figures, such as victims in terms of serial murder, emerge according to the nature of the task in which the organism is involved at the time. Anything that assists in the performance of the task becomes a figure. In the case of the serial killer, his task is to compensate for his feelings of incredibly low self-esteem, which he accomplishes by committing a murder. To achieve this task of alleviating his feelings of inferiority, he enters into a cycle of stages that compose a self-stimulating ritual. These expressions become figures for him. The choice of victim, as well as what he does to the victim, including all pre- and post-crime behaviour, are also regarded as figures for him.

Two types of figures exist: natural and unnatural. Natural figures are functionally embedded in the totality of the organism, while unnatural figures are those that become isolated from the organism. The latter are produced by traumatic events and repeated drills. Furthermore, natural figures represent a preference expressed by the person's own self, while unnatural figures are rigid and mechanical.

In the serial killer, we clearly see both natural and unnatural figures in action. The killer's known victim type and his signature are natural figures because they express his preferences. These are fixed and embedded within his psyche because they allow him to commit his crime in the way that is necessary in order for him to obtain satisfaction. His chosen method of disposal is also considered a natural figure.

In the life of any serial killer, we are able to see a series of traumatic events, which have contributed to his formation as a murderer. These are considered root causes within the medical model, and can lead to the disease of serial murder. Such causes often include a history of substance abuse, malnutrition, addiction, or any of the other manifestations discussed earlier. These events, and their psychologically damaging effects, are real and cannot be dismissed by either the killer or those who are trying to grasp a better understanding of him. These events have given rise to several unnatural figures within the serial killer's life, which include his method of murder. This becomes a ritual, which gets repeated with each crime in a mechanistic way.

In his Organismic Theory, Goldstein also attributes constancies to the organism. These include sensory threshold, intellectual characteristics and emotional factors. He makes the claim that these constancies are inborn and function as the very agents of behaviour. He also states that these constancies are influenced by experience. Therefore, their manifestation will always reveal the type of environment in which the organism grows and thrives. This often reveals the serial killer's experiences of abuse, violence and sexuality, which are also exhibited in his horrible crimes.

Goldstein postulates three different types of behaviour, each of which is manifest in all serial murderers. The behaviours include performance, attitude, and the feelings associated with inner experiences. By contrast, processes are considered to be bodily functions that are experienced indirectly. Goldstein further breaks down behaviour into concrete and abstract.

Concrete behaviours are automatic reactions to stimuli. Abstract behaviours are actions which are consciously performed by the organism in response to certain stimuli. When the serial killer is in the planning stages of his crime, he is performing a concrete behaviour because he is automatically reacting to the stimulus of feeling incomplete and worthless. The actual murder, however, is an abstract behaviour because the killer is acting consciously upon the stimulus – in this case, the victim.

The dynamic concepts in Goldstein's Organismic Theory are threefold. The first concept is the equalisation process, the second self-actualisation, and the third coming to terms with the environment in which these concepts are achieved. In the equalisation process, we are dealing with a readily available supply of energy, which is evenly distributed in normal organisms. The goal of a normal organism is to equalise its energy. The level at which all tension is balanced is representative of such equalisation. This centre enables the organism to effectively perform the task of coping with the world and its pressures, and of actualising itself in all future activities. When an organism has achieved equalisation, orderliness of behaviour is realised, despite the presence of stimuli that may be considered disturbing.

In the serial murderer, we are dealing with an abnormal organism, one which cannot and does not develop the appropriate methods for dealing with conflict. Therefore, he does not reach equalisation. The serial killer is constantly being bombarded by catastrophic and abnormal stimuli, which produce isolation and inner conflict. He is a victim of the often arbitrary changes of both the inner and outer worlds.

The different drives which a normal organism possesses, such as the sex drive, are manifestations of purpose, which is called self-actualisation in Goldstein's theory. The satisfaction of any need is a prerequisite for self-actualisation in any organism. It is the principle by which the organism becomes complete.

In the serial killer, the need which requires satisfaction is the need to inflict pain on and to exert control over another human being. By stripping another organism of its ability to self-actualise, the serial killer achieves self-actualisation. The only way for a serial killer to become a complete organism is to kidnap, rape, torture and murder another organism. It is a parasitic relationship.

Goldstein recognises the significance of the objective world as a source of disturbance, as well as a source of supply. The environment imposes upon the organism, by stimulating it so that its equalisation is disturbed. The environment also provides the organism with what it needs in order to equalise tension. The two functions interact with one another. A normal organism appreciates this interaction, respects it, and uses it to its advantage.

The serial killer, incapable of equalisation, cannot cope with the disturbance the environment imposes upon him. He does not know the appropriate ways to use the environment to obtain what he needs in order for him to survive. He is terrified of the environment that has caused him a perceived harm, and this leads him to isolate himself from it. This also promotes the emergence of violent fantasies to which he becomes addicted, thus leading him to commit heinous crimes.

If an individual is exposed to situations with which he can readily cope as a child, he will have a very good chance of developing into a normally functioning adult. As a problem arises, he will establish a successful way in which to deal with it. If the conditions of a child's environment, however, make it too difficult and traumatic for his capabilities, he will develop patterns that cause him to isolate himself. Consequently, his behaviour will deviate from that of a normal organism, which is by nature neither aggressive nor submissive. It is necessary, however, to be one or the other at certain times. In the case of the serial murderer, he has developed a habit of aggression that influences his psychological being in inappropriate ways; thus his actions are inimical to his becoming a normal person.

Goldstein also describes four distinct types of symptoms which correlate to those we find in the medical model of serial murder. They are:

1. Direct
2. Indirect
3. Symptoms due to catastrophic conditions
4. Symptoms due to fatigue and perseveration

Direct symptoms are those which result from a systematic disintegration of a function. They are developmental regressions. With direct symptoms, we see individuals reverting to primitive emotions and behaviours. Brain-injured organisms suffer from direct symptoms.

Indirect symptoms are produced by changes in the damaged area. A defective component leads to a generalised malfunctioning of other parts of the system with which it has an interdependent relationship.

Symptoms that are attributed to catastrophic events stem from the organism's attempt to protect itself against that particular catastrophe. In the case of the serial killer, we see a consistent pattern of abuse or neglect. The incidents of abuse are catastrophic events which the child carries with him into later stages of development and adulthood. By the time the serial killer has reached the killing phase, he has developed methods (symptoms) to aid him in protecting against further abuse, rejection and neglect. He protects against these forms of punishment by committing murder.

Symptoms stemming from fatigue and perseveration are also found in the serial killer. Fatigue can come from tasks that are beyond an organism's ability to perform. Therefore, the killer must develop a set of methods to make him appear as though he can complete the given tasks, especially if everyone around him is capable of completing the same tasks. The serial killer utilises a façade of normalcy to hide the fact that he is abnormal. He uses fantasy to further isolate himself from those who can perform the tasks that he cannot, because it makes him feel that he is competent to complete these tasks.

Though not all brain-injured organisms commit serial murder, this does not disprove the theory of the medical model.

There are multiple symptoms which the serial killer exhibits that other brain-injured organisms do not. It is this constellation of symptoms, combined with the effects of traumatic brain injury, which results in the formation of the serial killer.

Serial killers are beyond our known concept of the term 'insanity'. They are mutants who have a diagnosable medical disease, the symptoms of which are part of a large pool of negativity and abnormality. Their actions are indeed reprehensible, but they have not become what they are by choice. They are who they are because of the circumstances they have been forced to suffer. They act as they do in order to establish a delusional means for survival.

9. ARTHUR SHAWCROSS, THE GENESEE RIVER KILLER

Arthur John Shawcross was born on 6 June 1945 in Kittery, Maine. The Genessee River Killer, so named because he dumped the bodies of his victims along the Genessee River, confessed to murdering ten women. At his trial in Rochester, New York in November 1990, he was convicted of ten counts of second-degree murder, for which he received ten consecutive twenty-five-year sentences. He is currently serving his time at the Sullivan Correctional Center in Fallsburg, New York. Most of his known victims were prostitutes. But these were not his first murders, and nor is this the first time that Shawcross has served time in prison for murder. In 1972, Arthur Shawcross was convicted of murdering Karen Allen Hill; and although under suspicion, he was never charged with the murder of a young boy named Jackie Blake, who lived in the same neighbourhood as Shawcross. For the Hill murder, he was sentenced to a 25-year prison sentence, but was eventually paroled in March 1987.

At his 1990 trial, Shawcross and his defence team pursued an insanity defence based on the claim that while he had been committing the murders he had been suffering from multiple personality disorder. During taped interviews conducted in preparation for his trial, Dr Dorothy Lewis recorded Shawcross speaking in the voice of a thirteenth-century cannibal named Ariemes, who took responsibility for the murders. Dr Lewis stated that Shawcross had committed the murders to satisfy Ariemes's lust for blood.

Shawcross was an enigma to psychological specialists as well as criminal investigators. This was due, in part, to his passive demeanour and violent temper. It was this set of seemingly contradictory psychological characteristics that made it difficult for police to detect and apprehend him. His were not the typical lust murders which investigators were accustomed to seeing, but rather resembled the more traditional type of homicides which generally occur between friends and lovers. An enigma, even within the realm of serial murderers, Arthur Shawcross exhibited so much control over his victims and the crime scenes that law enforcement authorities were initially convinced that he was subduing his victims with a stun gun, which was later discovered not to be the case.

Arthur John Shawcross had spent years in therapy and had been evaluated countless times by prison psychiatrists, as well as by psychiatrists from various mental institutions and the United States Army, in which Shawcross had served for a period of time. Yet he was capable of escaping detection due to his variable range of emotional states and the ability to shift from one to another without the slightest hint of transition. Shawcross, as well as suffering from a wide range of other root causes of serial murder, was also the victim of a severe case of post-traumatic stress disorder. The source of this stress was directly related to a set of events which began in early childhood and continue even to this day. So pervasive were these stresses that Shawcross existed within a state of emotional paralysis. He was wholly unable to relate to anyone in a normal, healthy way. The events of his past also caused him to suffer from a specific form of amnesia, which prevented him from remembering any of the positive and healthy methods of interaction he had once learned. An inability to relate productively to others is one of the probable reasons that he was married three times.

Existing in only two psychological states – homicidal and non-homicidal – Shawcross's condition can be attributed to a series of root causes of serial murder. These include neurological, genetic, biochemical and psychophysiological factors, which left Shawcross an emotionally and relationally absent individual. To communicate with Shawcross is to see from the outset that everything he ever did and everything he continues to do is an instinctive act of self-preservation.

Due to extreme sexual, physical and emotional abuse, which he suffered at the hands of the women of his early childhood, Shawcross spent most of his life in a semi-conscious dream state. This led his appearance to be that of a slow, passive, dim-witted individual. The truth, however, is that Shawcross had lived with his fantasies for so long that they had become a reality from which he eventually constructed the entire matrix of his personal history. Dr Joel Norris created a term to fit Shawcross's unique psychological condition. Norris referred to Shawcross's condition as *pathologica fantastica*. The term refers to a set of experiences, either real or imagined, which are so wide ranging in both nature and intensity that they prevent anyone, no matter how well trained, from creating an accurate profile of the individual disorders themselves.

Making his condition even worse, he also suffered from other root causes of serial murder, such as poisoning and severe neurological damage. It is also believed that he suffered from kryptopyroluria, or medical cannibalism. Evidence for this will be revealed later.

I have discussed his crimes with him numerous times, and although he will lie about those details of them which are embarrassing or shameful, the details of his fantasies and the overall presentation of the crimes he chooses to discuss are consistent with the known facts.

At nine years of age, Shawcross was introduced to sex by his mother's sister, Tina. He claims that from that point on he has been obsessed with sexual activity in its various forms. Also at this age, Shawcross suffered a psychologically damaging event when his mother suspected his father of impregnating a woman during World War II. From that time forward, Shawcross no longer had a male role model to assist him with further development and was shunned almost totally by his mother. Because of the way his mother treated his father after the incident with the other woman, cursing him at every opportunity and striking him every time she believed he was so much as looking at another woman, Shawcross's father stopped being a male role model. Shawcross reports that he lost all respect for his father because of this.

As a result of his father's own abandonment of his masculinity, Arthur Shawcross, too, began to feel ashamed and humiliated at being male. These feelings blossomed during a critical period of Shawcross's development into manhood, but also allowed him the freedom he needed to enter the world of fantasy, which eventually completely destroyed his life and the lives of his victims.

Shawcross reports that he was beaten regularly by both parents throughout his childhood, sometimes for things that he did not do. He was beaten with a broomstick and belt, as well as fists, on an almost daily basis. Head injuries were another common occurrence in his young life. He was hit over the head with a stone during a fight with his cousins when he was eight years old, and received a concussion. The bump is still present. Shawcross states that after the incident, which required several dozen stitches to close, he was unable to rise after sitting down because he had lost the feeling below his waist. Once, while swimming in Lake Ontario following the injury, he sank below the surface of the water and went for several minutes without air. This happened as a result of his temporary paralysis.

While in high school, Shawcross was struck inadvertently in the front of the head with a discus thrown by another member of the school track team. He remained unconscious for several hours and recalled very little of the accident. Even after his release from the hospital, Shawcross remained disoriented and dizzy for days. Later, while working as part of a construction crew, he was struck in the head by a forceful blow from a sledgehammer. Again he had little memory of the accident and it took several hours for him to regain consciousness. The extended period of dizziness and disorientation again continued for days after his release from the hospital. During a stint at Fort Benning, Georgia, Shawcross fell off the top rung of a 40-foot ladder, resulting in another concussion, and during the war in Vietnam he was hurled through the windshield of a jeep in which he was a passenger, and took several days to regain consciousness.

These injuries, combined with the destruction of his home life and his lack of respect for his own masculinity, reduced not only his resilience but also his inability to deal with the earlier sexual abuses that he had suffered during childhood.

Masturbation was a fascination for Shawcross, and he began to engage in this activity almost obsessively after being sodomised and forced to perform oral sex with his aunt. His brother, James Shawcross, would inform their mother whenever Arthur masturbated in bed. She threatened to cut off his penis if she ever caught him. At the age of ten, Shawcross engaged in a sexual relationship with a boy named Michael. Shortly after the relationship began, Shawcross and Michael met a man who owned a farm, and the man introduced the young boys to the pleasure of having sex with sheep. Michael ran away after a few visits to the farm, while Shawcross continued to visit until he was fourteen years old. At about this time, he began having sex with his sister, his cousin, and another younger girl who lived nearby. Shawcross has made the bold claim that his sister enjoyed it because she never told their mother. He has also stated that he continues to fantasise about having sex with his sister, while in prison.

The sexual experiences of Arthur John Shawcross increased in their level of violence after he was raped by an older man at the age of fourteen. Because of the rape, Shawcross learned to associate shame with any pleasure derived from sexual activity. He attempted to satisfy his obsession with sex in many ways, but claims that he only began to associate sex with violence after he was raped. He accounts for this by explaining that the man who raped him also choked him during the sexual act. It was after this point that Shawcross could no longer gain pleasure from sexual acts unless he was inflicting pain upon himself or someone else.

The easiest way for Shawcross to act upon this relationship between sexual pleasure and violence was to practise with animals. He experimented with a chicken, a cow, a dog and a horse before trying to have sex with a person again. This time, he realised that he enjoyed sex with women more than he did with animals, as long as there was some sort of violence associated with it.

At fifteen, Shawcross committed his first burglary, a common precursor to more serious, violent crimes. At eighteen, he had his first serious relationship with a woman. She was twenty-seven. At nineteen, Shawcross married for the first time, and the couple had their first child in 1964. After the birth of his child, Shawcross began to solicit prostitutes for sex. He divorced his wife in 1968, after being drafted by the army. Before going to Vietnam, he developed a pattern of taking long walks by himself in an attempt to escape his problems. He claims that he could not even look at alcohol or cigarettes because the very sight of them made him sick.

The years that Arthur Shawcross spent in Vietnam were a turning point in his life. He was able to survive, while others around him were killed instantly or died slowly from various wounds sustained in the numerous battles in which he had fought. As he killed more and more people, his urge to continue to kill was at a premium. He acted upon this urge during his tour of duty, as well as after he was discharged. He became highly skilled at modifying weapons for special purposes and often went hunting during his tour of service. So adept was Shawcross at weapons modification that he discovered that by placing the tops, or nipples, of baby bottles over his M-16, he could muffle the sound almost completely. This newfound knowledge led Shawcross to roam the jungles on his own, during which time he killed every living thing in sight.

In February 1968, Shawcross saw one of his close friends die from a gunshot wound to the face. After returning from a rest and recuperation trip to Hawaii following the incident, Shawcross no longer followed any rules, and went off into the jungles to fight his own personal war. Shawcross claims that during one of his killing sprees he tasted human flesh. According to his story he murdered a young girl in a village and cooked part of her leg, roasting it over a fire and consuming it. Shawcross also engaged in acts of torture and rape during his time spent in Vietnam. His particular choice of victims was mostly prostitutes, who he claimed deserved to die. He justified these actions by stating that if he did not kill them first, they were certain to take his life. As the stress of the war continued to build, Shawcross would disappear for longer periods of time. Eventually, not even children were safe from his M-16.

While these stories may seem a bit far-fetched, the fact is that they are a reality for Arthur Shawcross. They became the basis for many of his later actions following the war. For this reason, they have to be taken seriously, whether they stem from fantasy or reality.

Shawcross believed that all the women in Vietnam were prostitutes. Misperceptions and memories continue to haunt him to this day, although the veracity of his experiences is impossible to judge. Whether his memories stem from fantasy or reality, it is not far-fetched to believe that Shawcross committed his murders along the Genessee River as a direct result of what he believes happened to him in Vietnam. His memories are so vivid and horrific that it is impossible for Shawcross to suppress them, even if that is what he would genuinely like to do. His actions, and the actions of other military officers in the Vietnam War, were motivated by revenge and hatred. Nothing made sense to Arthur Shawcross during this time, except the violence and his own unbridled ability to release the sexual tension he experienced as a direct result of it.

With an IQ measured at 95, Shawcross falls within the average range of intellect. However, there is a drastic difference between his verbal and performance IQ, a difference often associated with learning disabilities and acting-out behaviours. When taking tests and growing frustrated, Shawcross exhibits temper tantrums and is often on the verge of physical violence. Tests for paranoia and schizophrenia demonstrate that Shawcross has long been alienated from the rest of society, and particularly the percentage of the population that is regarded as behaving normally. Shawcross harbours strong resentment towards women and sees them as occupying either one of two positions: either they are good or they are evil. The women who are classified by Shawcross as evil are viewed as untrustworthy carriers of disease. Therefore, he finds them suitable foils on which to act out his fantasies of violence and execution.

Genetic tests performed on Shawcross revealed that he has an extra Y chromosome. Magnetic Resonance Imaging (MRI) further revealed that at the tip of his right temporal lobe is a small cyst filled with fluid. Such an abnormality has been associated with primal, animalistic behaviour, a type of behaviour that was clearly exhibited when he cut the vagina out of one of his victims. A sufferer of temporal lobe seizures, Shawcross exhibits such symptoms of greater mental impairment as impaired memory, seeing auras, and the ability to fall into an almost coma-like deep sleep. Moments prior to the commission of a murder, Shawcross would break out in sweat and his perception would explode into what he described as a blinding white ball of light. He would then strangle his victims to death before drifting into a deep sleep. This type of unconsciousness is common with post-seizure behaviour. When he woke up hours later, the memory of what he had done was nothing more than a blur.

Shawcross experienced dissociative states, during which he would hear his mother berating the women he was involved with. He would also hear her inform him that these women had to die because they were not good enough for him. His electroencephalogram (EEG), conducted by Dr Lewis, came back abnormal. It revealed paroxysmal, irritated patterns in the bifrontotemporal areas on the right side of his brain. Sharp spikes and waves, as well as bursts of waves, were revealed by the testing, all symptoms that are clearly associated with the medical model of serial murder. In addition to what has already been mentioned, Shawcross shows many other symptoms from the pool that indicates this disease, as outlined below.

Firstly, Shawcross frequently awakes with scratches on his arms, which are the result of his gouging himself in his sleep. This is either a sign of self-mutilation or a severe allergic reaction. Secondly, Shawcross shows an ability to vividly recall the details that led up to his commission of a crime and becomes excessively angry whenever someone interrupts or glosses over a detail. Thirdly, he records readings of 200 kryptopyrroles during biochemical tests related to stress. A measurement of five is normal, while a reading of ten is considered high. Shawcross's score of 200 is off the charts, and no matter how many times he is retested he never records a reading of less than 75.

Shawcross sleeps only three to four hours a day. Occasionally he goes without sleep for days, without showing the negative effects usually associated with sleep deprivation. Shawcross reports that he smelled urine in the period leading up to the murders, and also claims to have experienced a tingling sensation in his extremities prior to waking up with the dead body of a victim beside him. When he was free to roam society, he engaged in hyperactive and compulsive behaviour, including disappearing for long periods of time without afterwards being able to recall where he had been or what he had done.

Shawcross suffers from a diagnosed case of lead poisoning, which may be attributed to the time he spent in Vietnam, during which he slept in an ammunition box and ate food out of other lead boxes. Symptoms of lead poisoning often include hallucinations and a chronic inability to mediate between behavioural extremes.

The genetic, biochemical, neurological and psychological impairments that afflict Arthur Shawcross not only lend credence to the medical model of serial murder, but also provide us with valuable insights into the inner workings of this particular serial killer. Such a complex interweaving of influences can be expected to result in some sort of behavioural disturbance, and while biological influences do not control behaviour completely, the case of Arthur John Shawcross suggests that criminality does have its origins in biology to a greater extent than was previously believed.

Traditional research into the field of serial murder has generally focused on a single-factor approach. While it is true that serial killers do share certain characteristics, a failure to focus on the factors that do not separate them from society at large leaves us at a great impasse. The focus on separation from the public prevents us from painting a complete and accurate picture of this type of violent offender. Sociological factors, in combination with medical symptoms, provide the public with a greater understanding of this disease. Additional research into the medical model is not only called for but required. A thorough investigation is necessary if we are ever going to be able to fully understand the dynamism and complexity of the serial killer's true nature.

10. ROBERT JOE LONG

When I first began corresponding with Robert, also known as Bobby, Joe Long in the winter of 2002, he was initially reluctant about returning my letters with his own. In my first letter, I wrote to him about the medical model of serial murder proposed in this book. Having carefully studied his crimes and the circumstances which surrounded them for nearly an entire year, I was convinced that Long fitted the profile of this model and was anxious to offer him some new hope and explanations as to why he had committed the terrible acts which had become his calling card. In his first letter to me he wrote, 'Thanks for writing. I don't know how much help your information will be. No one has ever tried to understand me before and I don't understand myself. I'll have my lawyer look it over since he has a better knowledge of stuff like this. Thanks.'

From the content of that first letter, I surmised that Bobby Joe Long had been incarcerated for crimes he had committed, but that he did not understand them, and had been powerless against committing them. He sounded as though he, too, had abandoned all hope of ever finding answers to the questions that had plagued him and the families of his victims since his capture and arrest in July 1983. I suppose that any man, regardless of his crimes, who has spent nearly twenty years of his life behind bars, would have abandoned any hope of meaningful correspondence with someone on the outside. When you consider the fact that Long was one of the most dangerous serial killers of his day and that he romped in the same playground as Ted Bundy in his heyday, this becomes even clearer.

After several more letters in which Long discussed the quest for answers, he wrote, 'I wasn't always this way. Something snapped and died inside me after the accident and I couldn't control what I was doing. I knew it was wrong and wanted to stop, but couldn't. That's why I had to let them catch me. I thought that once that happened, I'd get the help I needed, but things didn't turn out that way.' Long recognised that he was sick and debilitated by a disease that had no name. He believed that if and when he was ever apprehended, doctors would be able to figure out what was wrong with him and could then provide him with the assistance he needed to right himself again. Unfortunately this did not happen, as is often the case within the narrow confines of the criminal justice system in the United States, which is more concerned with retribution and retaliation than rehabilitation and treatment.

Bobby Joe Long, serial rapist and murderer of at least nine victims, was born in Kenova, West Virginia, on 14 October 1953. By the time he was eleven years old, Long's breasts had begun to grow larger. It would later be determined that he suffered from a rare genetic disorder that produced excessive female hormones. Not only did the disorder cause Long's breasts to grow as they would in a young woman who was undergoing puberty, but his entire figure also started to change shape. Other members of his family also suffered from this dysfunction in the endocrine system. Long received prescription medication for the condition and also underwent surgery to have six pounds of tissue removed from his chest. Although this remedied the outwardly physical effects of the disorder to some degree, Long suffered from a lunar protomenstrual cycle for the remainder of his life.

In addition to his medical condition, Long grew up in a dysfunctional home environment, in which he was forced to sleep with his mother in her bed until he was thirteen years old. Bobby Joe Long endured a lifelong fear of being permanently transformed into a female, and this, along with other injuries he would suffer later in life, contributed to his formation into a serial killer. His mother divorced his father when he was very young, and Long was ripped away from his childhood roots and relocated to Florida. They were poor, and Long went undernourished and was forced to survive on unhealthy foods loaded with additives and preservatives, which may have contributed towards the development of poor brain chemistry. Long's mother was constantly changing jobs, which meant that they had to move on a regular basis throughout the state of Florida. As a result, Long never remained in one area long enough to establish any positive or lasting friendships. Additionally, Louella Long, Bobby's mother, was promiscuous and had numerous boyfriends wandering in and out of the rundown apartments and boarding houses she occupied with her son. This instability and lack of a positive male role model to demonstrate to an impressionable Long what it meant to be a man, and how to treat a woman as something other than property, also contributed to Long's serial rage.

The relationship between Bobby and Louella Long was further strained because Bobby had to rely solely on his mother for companionship, while she did not wish to spend any time with him at all. Long grew angry at the way his mother flaunted and gave herself to other men while virtually ignoring him, except when they were sharing the same bed. This rage was fuelled by Long's later head injuries and established for him a pattern of how to relate to members of the opposite sex. As for his relationship with his father, it was almost nonexistent. Between 1956 and 1968, Long and his father had contact on only a handful of occasions. When the elder Bobby Long did visit his ex-wife and son, he became violent and physically and sexually attacked Louella in front of their son, further embedding the belief that the only way to obtain a woman's attention and affection was to use violence. It was a dangerous lesson for a young child's troubled psyche.

Cindy Jean Guthrie entered Bobby Joe Long's life when he was thirteen years old and the two began dating. His mother, who had been his sole companion and the dominating force in his life up until this point, did not approve of the relationship.

Long ignored his mother's demands that he stop seeing Guthrie, and the two were married seven years after they met, when Long was twenty. Cindy Guthrie was as domineering as Louella, telling Bobby Joe what to do every chance she got. Both women also strongly resembled one another, being thin and fair. They furthermore sounded alike and were both manipulative. The relationship makes sense if you place yourself in Long's shoes, since being dominated by women was all he had ever known. It is interesting to consider that Long met Guthrie at the exact time that his mother met and later married her second husband.

Long excelled in school, even though he was constantly moving from one town to another. He had even been an apprentice electrician before joining the army to further his training in that field. Things were going as well as could be expected for Bobby Joe Long, and then it happened – the incident that would change his life forever and firmly cement him within the medical model of serial murder. Six months into his service in the military, Long was almost killed in a motorcycle accident. Doing nearly seventy miles an hour, Long slammed into a car. He was thrown from the bike and his helmet shattered when he made contact head-first with the other vehicle. His skull suffered a severe fracture and he remained in a semiconscious state for weeks following the wreck. When he finally recovered to an acceptable degree, Long suffered from terribly painful headaches and blurred vision. These two symptoms continue to plague him today. Despite the serious head trauma, neither Long's X-ray nor his EEG have ever been examined by a skilled neurologist.

This, however, had not been the first time that Long had suffered from head trauma. There are four other previously documented cases before Long had reached the age of ten that indicate that he had suffered severe brain damage in his youth. When he was five years old, he was thrown from a swing. A stick punctured his eye and became embedded in the medial portion of his eyelid. At the age of six, he was thrown off his bicycle. At seven, he was hit by the bumper of a car; and at eight, he was thrown off a horse. With each of these accidents, Long not only struck his head but remained unconscious for weeks afterwards. He also suffered from broken teeth, dizziness, blackouts, headaches and concussions. The cumulative result of these accidents alone, prior to the motorcycle crash, indicates that Long suffered from severe damage to his left temporal lobe, as well as damage to the surrounding areas of his central nervous system. This resulted in a loss of neurological functioning related to the sustained damage. An EEG taken later in his life revealed that he also suffered from a lesion on his left temporal lobe, which led to irregular muscle activity in his right leg and the right side of his face which persists to this day.

About the motorcycle accident, Long wrote, 'When I got out of the hospital I knew that there was something wrong with me because I couldn't stop thinking about sex. Day and night that's all I thought about, sex. I thought about having sex with anyone and everyone I saw and it drove me wild.'

A few months after the accident, Cindy Long gave birth to the couple's first child. While Bobby Joe Long has expressed feelings of joy about the birth, he claims that he was also plagued by the sexual problem he had experienced upon his release from the hospital. Long wrote that he and his wife were having sex at least twice a day, and even with that he had to constantly masturbate in order to get some relief from the sexual tension which had built up inside him. He wrote, 'I tried to tell the doctors about the sex and about the headaches that wouldn't go away even after I had taken a whole bottle of aspirin. I felt the side of my face go dead and started hearing noises that were much louder than what they actually were. Any sound at all was like a giant explosion ringing in my ears.'

Long also grew violent at the drop of a hat following the accident. Before wrecking the motorcycle, Long was known by family and friends as a laidback, easy-going guy. After the wreck, he grew violently out of control and flew into rages that he claims scared him nearly to death because he had never been so crazy before. What is even more indicative of the applicability of the medical model is that these violent urges would emerge out of nowhere, and once they were over Long would have no memory of them whatsoever, much like serial killer Arthur Shawcross.

After a split with the army over what Long says was mistreatment because he never received a complete medical diagnosis for his problems, he got work as an X-ray technician. But due to his explosively violent and unpredictable outbursts and because he was constantly making unwanted sexual advances towards female staff members, Long was released from several positions. As a result of the combined effects of his genetic abnormality, his temporal lobe damage, malnourishment, a divorce, and the negative way in which he viewed women, as well as an unhealthy compulsion with sex that led to fantasies about sexual intercourse, Long became the Classified Ad Rapist, and committed a series of at least 50 vicious rapes between 1980 and 1983. Long would phone the numbers listed in classified ads for furniture and other sale items, then make appointments to view the merchandise during the day, believing that the wives of the sellers would be home alone during this time. Once inside the homes of his victims, Long pulled out a knife, tied them up, then raped them and robbed their homes. His victims claimed that during the attacks he was never violent.

Long's fantasies about sex never involved violence while he was operating as the Classified Ad Rapist because the primary goal of these fantasies was to obtain sexual gratification, not to harm anyone. This period of time in Long's life was certainly a precursor to his later murders, as his fantasies and desires were no longer built around the simple act of sexual intercourse but required that a new level of danger be added to the equation in order for him to achieve some level of satisfaction. Ironically, Long was arrested and charged with rape in 1981 for an attack on a former girlfriend. Long never committed this crime, and after being convicted he received a new trial. This time the charges against him were thrown out, due to the fact that witnesses surfaced to corroborate his side of the story. Shortly after being released from prison, Long made a horrible mistake that would have a profound impact on his life and the lives of his victims. He went to see a doctor about his problems, but left the office shortly before his appointment because he feared that once he had told the doctor about the rapes and his sexual compulsion, he would be sent to jail. Soon afterwards, the murders began.

Long preyed on what he thought were 'loose' women, which is the same way he viewed his mother. He picked them up in bars or on the street, drove them to a secluded stretch of road in the countryside of Tampa, tied them up, raped them, strangled them, and dumped their bodies along the roadside. By this time Long's fantasies, probably as a result of a further deterioration of his already frail mental condition, turned to group sex and overpowering women, rather than simply having sexual intercourse to achieve gratification. After the commission of each crime, Bobby Joe Long would retreat to his apartment and sleep for as long as twelve hours. When he woke up, he wondered if he had just dreamed the murders or if he had actually committed them. To answer his questions, he began to read the newspaper carefully and followed the story of his crimes religiously in the press. By November 1983, Bobby Long was in a deep depression, resting precariously on the bottom rung of the downward spiral of violence experienced by all serial killers when their fantasies completely engulf them and they can no longer gain the same level of satisfaction by committing the same types of crimes. He had committed eight murders and was disgusted with each of them. He was also disgusted with himself, but was powerless to eject himself out of the cycle of homicidal rage that had festered inside him for years, and which had been brought to the forefront of his life as a result of the terrible motorcycle accident he had experienced.

But Long did not kill every one of his victims. The woman he released was, at least in Long's mind, different from the other victims he had snuffed out. She had not fought back. She had talked to him like he was a real person, which was something that he had not experienced before. She had shared personal information about her life with him, and although he had raped her, he made the conscious decision to end his reign of terror and allow her to live. Long dropped the girl off in the same spot where he had picked her up, knowing and hoping that she would bring the police back to him. He had several opportunities to leave the Tampa area, even before this latest abduction and rape. The papers had informed him that a task force had been set up and was actively searching for the killer. He could have taken off to some other city, and if he had done so he probably would not have been apprehended in his lifetime. But as he explained in a letter to me, 'I could have ran [sic], sure, but for what? I wanted to stop. I could have got away with it, but I was sick and didn't want to hurt anyone else. I hoped I'd get some help, but not running when I could have didn't get me anything but locked up and forgotten about.' Long has expressed constant anger over the fact that he did the right thing by not running away when he could have done. He also expresses anger about not receiving proper treatment for his condition.

Bobby Joe Long was arrested outside a movie theatre as he was exiting the show. Once at the station, he confessed to his crimes. In 1985 a psychological examination revealed that Long was competent to stand trial because he knew the moral implications of his actions. He was charged with nine counts of murder and numerous other felony counts for abduction, rape and sexual assault. He was convicted and sentenced to die.

While an EEG was performed during Long's psychological evaluation, the results reported to the court were superficial because they did not cover the entire 36-hour period required to detect a deep brain dysfunction. Long was also bound in shackles at the time of the exam, so no neurological reflex tests could be conducted. Bobby Joe Long is a classic example of the medical model of a serial killer. He suffered from malnourishment as a child, which led to the development of poor brain chemistry. He suffered several head traumas, including damage to the frontal lobe of his brain, and also suffered from other forms of brain damage that were left untreated and combined with his view of women and the intermingling of sex and violence to create a serial killer.

The story of Robert Joe Long and his victims is a tragic one indeed. Plagued by several disabilities, most severely the brain damage he was forced to live with from the age of five, Long knew all along that his murderous spree was wrong, but could not stop it himself without some form of outside intervention. He continually writes that he believes that his brain is dried up and dead, but it will only be after he is executed that someone will finally take notice of that, and by then it will be too late. Long has never stated that he belongs anywhere other than where he is. I think that most of us would strongly agree with that. The fact that he suffers from a medical disease does not mitigate the fact that he should be punished for his crimes. However, we cannot overlook that fact that he seems to have intentionally let one of his victims go free for a reason. If he had not done so, he probably would have continued to rampage through Tampa, claiming dozens of additional victims. If he had left Tampa for some other locale, the body count would also have risen. Long, however, chose with the last bit of humanity still inside him to get caught, hoping that he would obtain the help he had so desperately sought from the army as well as his wife and others. Unfortunately he did not receive it. The criminal justice system has not, and probably never will, provide him with the answers and treatment he requires in order to finally come to grips with the terrible things he has done.

11. THE NARCISSISTIC PERSONALITY THEORY

Narcissistic Personality Disorder is not in itself dangerous. Its prevalence is less than 1% of the general population, with the majority of this group considered harmless. Because people suffering from the disorder rarely express a potential for violence, it is not commonly associated with aggressive behaviour. But as with any other disorder, an unhealthy combination of factors can turn something innocuous into something volatile. The disorder can lead to a deadly manifestation in certain individuals, and is in fact present in many serial killers.

To begin with, it is a personality disorder. By definition, this means that it is characterised by a recurring pattern of maladaptive social behaviour. According to the American Psychiatric Association's *Diagnostic and Statistical Manual of Mental Disorders* (1994), a personality disorder can be demonstrated by problems with cognition, affect, interpersonal functioning or impulse control. Several different personality disorders exist. To simplify diagnosis, they are arranged in clusters according to similarity. The dramatic and emotional nature of Narcissistic Personality Disorder places it in the same categorical cluster as several other personality disorders. Some of these disorders are more prevalent, and perhaps more familiar. Antisocial and Borderline Personality Disorders are much more common, and share similar features with Narcissistic Personality Disorder.

The specific features of Narcissistic Personality Disorder include 'a pervasive pattern of grandiosity (in fantasy or behavior), a need for admiration, and a lack of empathy' (American Psychiatric Association, 1994). The characteristics are present by early adulthood, at which time the disorder can be diagnosed. It develops over an extended period of time and is generally considered to be the product of persistent difficulties in the home environment, including problems with the primary support group. In this case, absentee parents are just as problematic as parents who are physically abusive. The prognosis for any type of personality disorder is not encouraging. Most psychologists favour an approach that focuses on the management of symptoms, rather than the improbable prospect of a full recovery. The impairment becomes so rigidly ingrained that it defines the person's very character, hence the term 'personality disorder'.

Serial killers are usually diagnosed with Antisocial Personality Disorder, and who can argue? A person who commits the most heinous of crimes is certainly a sociopath. He has no respect for authority, and nor does he perceive how the rights of others are equal to his own. He is, by his very nature, a predator. The prison system is filled beyond capacity with his type. A casual glimpse into his past will probably reveal that he has more than once been in trouble with the law. Common indicators from childhood include fighting, breaking and entering, fire-setting, theft, substance abuse, and even cruelty to animals. He lacks a conscience and forms an addiction to thrill-seeking activities. While all these factors contribute to the Antisocial Personality diagnosis, they do not provide a complete picture: certain features are missing. Because Narcissistic and Antisocial Personality Disorders belong to the same categorical cluster, they share common symptoms. The advantage of the Narcissistic Personality diagnosis, however, is that it recognises other salient factors. These factors offer a better set of details than the Antisocial Personality diagnosis, defining how a serial murderer is influenced by his environment, as well as how he is programmed to interact with it.

Beyond the typical manifestations of antisocial behaviour, the serial killer is driven by an excessive need for attention. Often, this attention begins with a captive audience – his victims. But while this may be good enough to begin with, he soon graduates to need further attention from a larger audience. After all, his victims do not live to tell others about him. The type of recognition he gets from them can only be temporarily sustained. Once a victim has been killed, the killer must find another one to satisfy his growing need for attention. Alternatively he may try to find another way to expand his audience: positioning victims' bodies for easy discovery or maximum shock effect is one such method. But this still does not provide the desired amount of attention. After all, he cannot take credit for what he has done, for to do so would be his undoing. Therefore, he must find other ways to receive acknowledgement.

Often, he will inject himself into the police investigation of his own case. He may masquerade as an investigator and make phone calls to surviving family members and other civilians associated with the case. This action is often misinterpreted as an attempt to discover if the investigation is getting too close. It is actually a form of self-gratification for the killer, in which he is fascinated by the attention he has created and desires to know what the rest of the world knows. In some cases, he is brazen enough to jokingly admit to his crimes, or to conduct a face-to-face interview with a member of the victim's family or one of her friends. All the while, he continues to pretend that he is an undercover officer of the law. John Norman Collins, the Michigan Murderer, arrived at a funeral home where one of his victims was being prepared for burial, and asked to take a picture of the badly decomposed body. The Happy Face Killer, Keith Hunter Jesperson, sent letters to the press declaring himself to be the guy they were after, and signed these letters with a smiley face. A grandiose need for attention is the primary characteristic of Narcissistic Personality Disorder. The killer contacts the media to 'play up' the attention he has generated. He also challenges the authorities and defies them to catch him. He is better than everyone else, and to prove it he will not get caught.

But most of the time, he does get caught. His overbearing need to be recognised for his crimes almost guarantees that he will inject himself too deeply into the investigation to escape suspicion. After all, he is his own biggest fan. And once apprehended, he will continue to believe in his own misguided sense of superiority and invincibility. Serial killers often demand to represent themselves during their trials. Serving as their own counsel, they have been responsible for some of the most outlandish theatrics ever to disgrace a courtroom. Gary Heidnik, for example, claimed that the bodies found in his basement were already there when he bought the house.

People with Narcissistic Personality Disorder expect others to co-operate with them. When this does not happen, it shatters the illusion of the influence they perceive themselves to have over others. They will react with extreme prejudice towards anyone they feel has betrayed them. Numerous examples can be cited in which a serial killer expected an accomplice not to testify against him, even though such testimony would guarantee a lighter sentence for the accomplice. As will be seen in the next chapter, such situations seldom unfold in the way the serial killer expects them to. To truly comprehend how serial killers can believe something so delusional, it is useful to consider how they view interpersonal relationships. They choose their relationships according to anticipated gains. In other words, they become involved with people who are easily persuaded. Ideal partners are those who are always willing to accept blame and criticism. But more importantly, these partners are eager to please. They will often assume responsibility for financial payments and other material expenses. This is a direct manifestation of the narcissistic belief that others owe them something.

Because of the belief that others owe them, people with Narcissistic Personality Disorder are often under-employed relative to their ability. They tend to rely on the fantasy that their importance will be duly recognised. As a result of this elevation in status, they should get promoted. But because this never happens, they often seek revenge through stealing. In their minds, however, they are only taking their just deserts. No employer appreciates a worker who steals from the company, but theft often goes undetected. This is probably because the narcissistic personality is obsessed with its own self-image. In addition, the majority of people with this disorder are intelligent. They generally display an IQ score that is in the average to above-average range. Their job performance, however, seldom matches their ability. They are unwilling to work for things that they feel should just be handed to them. An ironic observation is that these individuals are willing to expend a maximum amount of energy in finding ways to avoid performing work-related responsibilities, when to simply perform these responsibilities would require significantly less effort. They are also masters at deceiving others into believing that they are busy. But to people with Narcissistic Personality Disorder, it is all about appearances and manipulation.

The same thing that is true of a serial killer's work history is also true of his social and intimate relationships. They are marked by a selfish capacity to promote appearances and manipulate others to his advantage. Relationships are built to gain something, and are maintained for as long as they serve this purpose. According to the *Diagnostic and Statistical Manual of Mental Disorders*, others who relate to them 'typically find an emotional coldness and lack of reciprocal interest' (1994). Exploitation is the order of the day. As long as a person continues to meet a perceived need, the killer will maintain the relationship (unless, of course, the need is to kill the person). Some killers are so certain of their ability to control others that they recruit them to assist in committing murder. While this poses an obvious risk, a narcissistic personality insists that his partner would never turn him in. And why wouldn't he believe this, when he so strongly presumes to have control over others? He believes that he is not capable of making a foolish decision, one that could put his very life in jeopardy.

A serial killer who operates with a partner is twice as likely to get caught as one who works alone. Considering their inability to maintain long-lasting relationships, the odds are even better. What is to stop the partner from cancelling the relationship and going to the police? And if the partner gets caught, what is to stop him or her from turning state's evidence in exchange for a lighter sentence? When asked why he had decided to take such a risk, serial killer Douglas Clark denied any involvement in the series of murders for which he was convicted. Instead he put the blame on his partner, Carol Bundy. He explained it to me in the following way:

> I was never interested in Bundy. I was repelled by her. I ignored her. I left her 'free rent, food, car-use' lodging to pay rent with other women. I told her in a letter or two, I feel she's fucking lucky I'm not the killer/partner she describes. Had it been me, I'd have whacked her depraved ass August 9, or even long before. She's a crazy acting, loud person. Anyone even 1% sane and intelligent would have had to know this crazy bitch can't keep her compulsively yammering mouth shut. So, use your experience and training – Why would I do this? Why would I tell a crazy motor-mouth drama queen I can't stand to live with 'free'? Why not whack her, if so, as a liability?

The explanation serves a dual purpose. First, it demonstrates that Clark would have considered it a poor choice to include a partner in his crimes. Since he is incapable of having made the glaring mistakes that led to his arrest, it must have been someone else that assisted the self-confessed partner. Second, if it had been him, he would certainly have been smart enough to protect himself by eliminating any potential threat of being discovered. In other words, he would have killed his partner! Since this was not done, he could not possibly have been involved. Therefore, the crimes must have been committed by someone else, someone who was a complete idiot, someone who was nothing like him.

The question remains – why do so many serial killers choose to work with a partner? By now, the answer should be clear. As narcissistic personalities, they believe that others can be manipulated. They convince themselves that they have control, and inflate their sphere of influence to imaginary proportions. Attention they get from the media does not help. Likewise, neither does the fan mail that arrives once they are caught. Clark has been on death row for over 23 years, yet he continues to receive a steady stream of letters from various female admirers.

In the trial of a serial killer, another feature of Narcissistic Personality Disorder becomes glaringly apparent – his contempt for anyone who does not support him. Consider the case of the Night Stalker, Richard Ramirez. His reaction to being found guilty for a string of first-degree murders was to lash out at the jury, 'You maggots make me sick. I will be avenged. Lucifer dwells within all of us!' Because they perceive others to be inferior, they feel entitled to especially favourable treatment and expect to be granted special privileges. When these expectations are not met, they often become furious, and respond with unmitigated anger. It is no wonder they have taken the lives of others.

The average serial killer is intelligent. That being the case, how does he get caught? What disadvantages does he suffer? He certainly feels that he cannot be stopped. And this is the very thing that serves as his biggest impediment – an over-inflated sense of self that assures him that others will never measure up to him. Try as they might, they are not smart enough to catch him. He constantly devalues and underestimates the abilities of others. Such faulty thinking will lead him to act with overabundant confidence. As a result, he will operate more freely and with less caution. He might even purposefully plant cryptic clues. One of these mistakes will be his undoing. But once he is caught, it is still not over. In his mind, he maintains that he did not get caught. Because he is unstoppable, he will not be able to accept that it has ended. This explains why so many death row inmates continue to proclaim their innocence. In their minds, they did not get caught; getting caught implies that they have done something wrong. Instead, the cops caught the wrong guy! Once again, the killer portrays himself as the victim.

Silent victims they are not. They want the world to know that they have been persecuted. Getting caught is a mixed blessing. On the one hand, they do not want to pay the steep penalty that accompanies their crimes; but on the other, they are finally getting the recognition they have always wanted. And while it is difficult to strike a satisfactory compromise between these urges, the need for attention is so excessive that some researchers have suggested that serial killers want to get caught. While this is not true of most killers, perhaps it is the reason why some of them have given themselves up. For people who are otherwise unremarkable, it does afford them the recognition of holding a frightening place in our memories.

The serial killer's narcissistic behaviours arise out of the need to feel important. Although he presents a clever and confident persona, his gruesome activities are the result of low self-esteem. He compensates for these feelings in the most extreme ways. It is highly unlikely that he is the product of a nurturing environment, and a close investigation of his formative years will characteristically reveal something traumatic or severely lacking. These things are usually easy to identify, but in some cases surprisingly little can be detected – perhaps because families who experience dysfunction tend to guard their secrets closely. No one wants to be associated with the type of problems that may have contributed to the formation of a serial killer. Even so, the problems usually attract the attention of some investigators in the media. But as you will see in the next chapter, even those who have lived a rather privileged life can be candidates for this crime. They may believe that they can escape accountability, but public outrage makes it difficult to get away with murder.

Because a serial killer is narcissistic by nature, he may believe in a 'manifest destiny' to kill. Because he regards himself as being above all others, he has the right to decide who may live, and who should die. In short, he enjoys playing God. Others should make the ultimate sacrifice for him. But this not only applies to victims: it is also true of those who may be recruited to assist him. The following chapter examines a killer who was not satisfied with sacrificing several victims of his own. To prove his supremacy, he recruited a partner and demanded the ultimate expression of loyalty – he found the perfect match and groomed her to kill for him.

12. DOUGLAS CLARK, THE SUNSET STRIP SLAYER

1980 was a frightening year for the residents of Los Angeles. An explosion of homicides marked the calendar. Never before had the city experienced more than a thousand murders in a single year, and it would not happen again until more than ten years later, by which time the city's population had increased by over half a million. It did little to calm the collective fear when serial murderers like the Trash Bag Killer, the Freeway Killer and the Hillside Stranglers had only recently been making headlines. Add to this list one more killer, the Sunset Strip Slayer, and the situation appeared to be an epidemic.

Douglas Daniel Clark was born in Pennsylvania in 1948. While it is easy to trace his family's movements from one exotic location to the next (his father was stationed in the navy), few details of his childhood and adolescent years are known. After 23 years of 'playing amateur psychologist' with people who have attempted to analyse him, Clark remains evasive about his past. In a recent interview he stated, 'Maybe someday psychologists will be able to figure out the slightest fraction of 1% of human behavior.' Of the two psychiatrists who formally evaluated him, he added, 'They were a couple bottom feeders who billed 3–4 times the number of jail visits that actually occurred.' For a man who has a lot to say about others, he does not choose to reveal much about himself, except when attempting to glorify certain 'heroic' accomplishments. In a similar vein, he also refuses to acknowledge any responsibility for the Sunset Murders. Ironically, the one thing that has put this attention-seeker in the public spotlight is the very thing he most vehemently denies.

Before examining the narcissistic character of Douglas Clark, it is necessary to discuss the crimes that put him on the map.

After all, the signatures of these murders are an expression of his psyche. While it is suspected that he killed at least two people during April 1980, his first known victim was Marnett Comer. She was a seventeen-year-old runaway from Sacramento who had been picked up by Clark on 31 May. As soon as he pulled a .25-caliber handgun on her, she realised it had been a mistake to get into the car with him. The next morning, the blue Datsun had a cracked gearshift and a peculiar indentation on the passenger-side door panel.

Two weeks later, Clark told his girlfriend, Carol Bundy, about what had happened. The girl he had picked up had panicked when she saw the gun. In her attempt to escape, she kicked the gearshift. He explained that she had become so out of control that he had been obliged to shoot her, which was where the indentation in the door panel had come from. Bundy recalled how a similar thing had happened in April, when Clark had returned home with blood on his hands and face. He had handed her a bloody knife and a story about having been attacked. After cleaning the knife for him, she had noticed a tiny puddle of blood underneath the seat of their Buick station-wagon. It occurred to her that he might be using both vehicles for urban hunting expeditions. She also began to speculate about the real reason why he had wanted her to buy a matching pair of handguns. The amazing thing is that she willingly decided to go along with his incredible explanations.

The next two victims were stepsisters. On 11 June, Clark spotted sixteen-year-old Cynthia Chandler and fifteen-year-old Gina Marano. He invited them into his car and drove to a vacant lot, where he pulled a gun on them and ordered Marano to look away as he forced Chandler to give him oral sex. Although he shot both girls, neither died right away. He drove them to a rental garage, where he attempted to have sex with Chandler's now-dead body. He then waited for Marano to die, before sodomising her. He left their bodies in the garage, but returned later that evening after having dinner with a girlfriend named

Lydia Crouch. Before leaving her house, he asked to borrow her Polaroid. After engaging in further necrophilic acts, he wrapped the bodies in a blanket and drove them to an area near the Disney studios, where he dumped them down the side of an embankment at an on-ramp of the Ventura Freeway. It is widely assumed that he did not know the identities of these victims, and although he admitted to knowing Chandler, little corroborating evidence was made available in court. But when I commented on the tragic loss of these attractive girls, he responded:

> Cindy was cool – a girl you didn't take a shower while she and your wallet were in the room, unguarded – but, cool. She was a 'hitch-hooker' when I met her. She never let it 'slip' as to where she was from, or how old she really was – she played 19 with such casual skill. She'd let you know, honestly or not, what she needed – a motel a few days, $20 to pay back a friend, etc. She'd not relax into a 'consent to sex' mode until you either met her goals, or let her know a good reason why she can't have all that. Then she'd always take what she could get and act bored. I assumed she was possibly not 19, but few 30-year-old, simple women are that refreshingly adult.

As to why he chose to reveal this information, the answer is simple. He wanted others to feel envious of him. In an egocentric, selfish way, he wanted the world to know that he had taken something that no one else could ever have. It is the same from the victim's point of view. She would never have a comparative experience with another man.

Other women also fell victim to this depraved thought process. On 20 June, Clark invited his obliging girlfriend, Carol Bundy, to join him in the hunt for a new victim. Identified only as 'Cathy', their next victim was picked up on Highland Avenue in Hollywood. In what was perhaps a test of loyalty, or an attempt to secure insurance against being turned in, Clark arranged for Bundy to pull the trigger on this one. Watching from the back seat while Cathy performed oral sex on Doug, Carol waited anxiously for the right moment. Clark, however, became impatient and waved his fingers for the gun. She handed it to him. Cathy suddenly became aware that something was wrong. Although his arm was still in an awkward position from retrieving the gun, Clark pulled the trigger and shot her. Cathy struggled to continue breathing, while Bundy quickly moved to the front seat to conceal what was going on. After covering the victim's blood-soaked head with a jacket, they drove to the Santa Clarita Valley. It was not until 3 March the following year that her body was discovered, with the remains found beside a remote stream in Bouquet Canyon. Her true identity is still unknown. Referred to as 'Cathy' by the perverted couple who took her life, the Los Angeles County Sheriff's Department identified her as Jane Doe no. 28.

On 21 June, the depravity continued to escalate. Clark picked up a prostitute named Exxie Wilson. She had recently moved from Little Rock, Arkansas with her friend, Karen Jones. Jones had dropped out of college to make a living in the same profession as her friend. She considered it a practical alternative to the other available forms of work, as she was supporting a young son. Clark had seen both women together, but continued to prowl for a lone victim. When he noticed them working separately later, he propositioned Wilson to get in the car, and drove to an empty parking lot behind the Studio City Sizzler. While Wilson was performing oral sex on him, he shot her in the back of the head. Although he was careful about the angle of trajectory, Wilson bit down on him as she was dying. He quickly dragged her from the car and stripped her, then foraged through the 'kill bag' that Bundy had conveniently put together for him. Still enraged that he had been bitten, he took a knife from the bag and proceeded to decapitate Wilson. He put the head in a plastic bag and tossed it on the floor behind the passenger seat. He left her body in a spreading pool of blood as he drove away from the parking lot. Concerned that Wilson's friend might be able to identify him, he began searching for her. He found Karen Jones waiting for her friend in the same general vicinity, and convinced her to get in the car with him. He must have found it amusingly ironic that the head of the woman she was searching for was only inches from where she was sitting. He pulled up near the Burbank studios, where he put a bullet in her left temple. After taking her cash, he pushed her body from the car and drove back to his apartment.

Carol Bundy could not wait to hear about her boyfriend's latest hunting expedition. She would get more than a story, however, when she arrived to find a severed head sitting on the kitchen sink. Clark bragged about having taken it into the shower with him, where he had used it to simulate oral sex. They kept it for five days, during which time it was stored in the freezer. Making plans to shock the world, he suggested that she put make-up on it. It seemed like a good idea, until he realised that fingerprints might be found in the cosmetics. He ordered her to scrub it clean, then placed it in a wooden treasure box that she had bought specially for the occasion. They drove to an alley behind Hoffman Street, less than a mile from where he had killed her, and Bundy gently tossed the box from the car. It cracked when it hit the pavement, but its contents did not spill out. They drove off. Early the following morning, a young man returned home to find the box blocking his parking space. He was understandably horrified when he opened it. The medical examiner was able to determine that it had recently been frozen. When he stuck a thermometer into its neck, the temperature read 35° Fahrenheit – the outside temperature was 65°. Moreover, he was able to determine that it had not been sitting in a box on the asphalt for very long. Whoever was behind the murder could not be very far away.

Doug Clark had no intention of leaving his Verdugo apartment. Not only was he living in a place where Bundy paid the rent, but he had also met an eleven-year-old girl, who he was able to groom for purposes of sexual gratification. A typical paraphiliac with multiple tendencies toward necrophilia and paedophilia, he clearly suffered from feelings of inadequacy and low self-esteem. By engaging in sexual acts with those who could not form a basis for comparison, he would not have to encounter embarrassment. But as his sickness grew, so did his carelessness.

The body of his first known victim, Marnett Comer, had been found on 30 June in a north San Fernando Valley ravine. A hunter out looking for snakes stumbled upon an old mattress. Lifting it with a stick, he found a body underneath. It had remained in the summer heat for an entire month. Because of indirect exposure to the elements, it had been naturally mummified. It had also been slit down the middle. But despite the latest grisly discovery, Clark went searching for another victim with the eleven-year-old in tow.

On 1 August, they went out cruising. She helped him pick the next victim. Although she watched from the back seat while the woman performed oral sex on Clark, he decided it was too risky for her to witness an execution. He took the young girl home, then drove away with the woman. He would later tell Carol Bundy that he shot this victim in the back of the head while she was giving him oral sex. Afterwards, he drove her body to the water towers in Antelope Valley, where he positioned it in the trunk of the car to have sex with it. He then discarded the body and drove home. But Bundy was unimpressed that she had been replaced by an eleven-year-old accomplice. She intended to do something about it.

In a desperate attempt to win Clark's admiration, Carol Bundy decided to show him that she was not the incompetent accomplice that he had claimed her to be. She took the eleven-year-old girl to meet a former lover named Jack Murray. Using the girl as bait, she enticed him into the back of his van. She permitted him to fondle the girl, but would not allow him to have sex with her. Returning the next day, she showed Murray the 'kill bag' and disclosed that her current boyfriend was the Sunset Strip Slayer. She begged him to help her decide what to do. He agreed. Bundy wondered if he might do her another favour. She asked him for sex, saying that she would allow him to have the eleven-year-old if he consented. Murray climbed into the back of his van, where Bundy shot him in the back of the head twice. She then took the knife out of the kill bag and proceeded to stab him repeatedly in the buttocks. After carving around his anus, she realised that the bullets in his head could be traced to a .25 caliber gun, so she decapitated him. She took the trophy to show to Clark.

He was not as supportive as she had hoped, berating her for having left the shell casings in the back of the van. Together, they drove around until they found a trash can near Griffith Park, where she discarded Murray's head. By this time, she began to realise that the relationship was hopeless. When police found Murray's bloated body in the back of his van on 9 August, Bundy was added to the list of suspects. She was questioned by police, and stuck to the alibi that Clark had worked out for them. But with the pressure mounting, his criticism had become intolerable. She went to work the next day and reported the murders to a couple of co-workers. By the time her shift had ended, police were already on their way. She and Clark were arrested. Although Clark attempted to recant the alibi he had given to Bundy, it was too late. She had told the police everything.

Following up on leads she provided, police soon discovered the body that Clark had deposited near the water tower. As they were unable to link her to any missing persons, she was identified as Jane Doe no. 18. A bullet retrieved from the skull matched Clark's .25-caliber gun. Two days later, on 28 August, the remains of another victim were found in the Malibu Mountains, near Tuna Canyon. Bundy remembered the location as a dump site that Clark had pointed out during one of their summer drives. She was called Jane Doe no. 99. Although the bullet retrieved from her skull was the correct caliber, an incomplete jacket made it impossible to match it to a specific gun. Clark was convicted on six counts of first-degree murder on 28 January 1983. Three weeks later, he was sentenced to death row.

In the search for what produces a killer like Douglas Clark, not many answers can be found. His childhood reveals a life of privilege, in which physical abuse was absent. He was insulated from poverty, and neither parent instilled a zealous religious background. In fact, they were fiercely independent – and herein lies part of the answer. They were emotionally distant and socially isolated. They were international travellers and residents, and wherever they went they expected preferential treatment. Often living among indigenous people in areas such as the Marshall Islands, India, Venezuela and Western Australia, they lived a life of colonial privilege and elevated status. Local servants often took care of the family's household tasks. It was a life unlike any other in modern American times.

Young Douglas was enrolled in the finest international and private schools. He attended Ecolat in Geneva, Switzerland. Reserved for children of UN diplomats, royalty and various celebrities, it was also a place where students were required to live away from home. Although he enjoyed it, he managed to get into a considerable amount of trouble. He desperately wanted others to be envious of him. As such, he often tape-recorded his sexual exploits with the town girls to play back to his classmates. Commenting on those days, he said, 'Boarding schools are like summer camp, a bit. Nothing too unusual. I did have a nice time, and enjoyed when girls' schools sent buses full of equally hormonal teens to dances.' And if these girls did not provide enough entertainment, he could always set his sights on the women who taught at the school. He once wrote an erotic letter to a female teacher. In addition to multiple incidents of theft and drunkenness, this was enough to have him expelled. Perhaps the dean of student affairs would have looked upon it differently if Douglas had produced some academic effort, but as it was he could not be bothered to do the work. Although his parents were forced to come and get him, neither of them would admit that he had shown any behavioural problems. It was this pattern of denial that cultivated a young man who would refuse to accept any responsibility for his actions.

Beneath the surface of a spoiled brat, however, lurked a lonely and detached boy. His parents could not be bothered with his amateur charades for attention. Like many neglected children, he learned quickly that his parents would only respond whenever he got into serious trouble. At such times, they would defend him against any insult. It was a lesson that he put to his advantage. But other times, he delighted in the freedom he experienced at the conditioning of permissive parents. It was during several adventurous adolescent outings that he developed a morbid fascination with inanimate bodies. One of the earliest experiences of this included a time when he explored a garbage dump on the island of Kwajalein. With his brother's .22 rifle in hand, he shot a bunch of rodents. He recalled, 'I shot 100s of rats, in the dump, as a kid, but once I saw the actual bodies we teens had created, one day, I never again fired a gun at a living thing.' Assuming this was truly an aversive reaction, one wonders what station the prostitutes on Sunset Strip must have occupied in his mind.

Even more telling is the period he spent in India during his formative years. Operating under a strict caste system, the country was a fascinating place for an American family to enjoy, but it was not a place' where the impoverished multitudes received a fair standard of living. Every morning in Calcutta, for example, bodies of the poor who had died of exposure were routinely shovelled off the streets. Retrospectively looking at his fascination with necrophilia, I inquired if he had ever seen the deceased bodies of the poor. He had. Reflecting on these experiences, he admitted:

They did routinely collect dead from the streets, and the people who could pay had carts come for theirs. But hey, in any city that size, 1/45th of the populace dies every year. Do the math, everyone has to die somewhere. They did really set pyres on the steep banks of the Ganges in Benares, been there, seen it – Clark's Hotel (got an ashtray? I smoked already). They let some of the less rich persons they knew, usually, put a few bodies wrapped in white gauze on the fire as it got going. Some rich folks held weekly pyres for families of 'workers', too. My mom found a Polaroid of me with a 60 lb python around my shoulders, and I was grounded for a week. She *didn't* find the ones of the Clark's Hotel's fine menu of girls.

It seems he had already developed a taste for erotic fantasies involving corpses at a young age. It is notable that he often posed the bodies of his victims and preserved these images in photographs. In fact, he positioned stepsisters Marano and Chandler in all sorts of deviant positions, including placing each one of their heads in the other's pubic area. Perhaps his earlier encounters with inanimate bodies had a great deal to do with his later obsessions. After all, it can be presumed that his earliest exposure to nude female bodies involved corpses.

Narcissistic features can be present in childhood, but the disorder cannot be formally diagnosed until adulthood. I met Clark when he was 53 years old. His correspondence reveals relatively little about his involvement in the Sunset Strip murders. In fact, he emphatically denies killing anyone. But it is what is *not* present in his letters that is most revealing. Not only does he vacillate between anger and righteous indignation, but he also displays a complete lack of empathy. He does not express any concern for others. He possesses a high IQ, and his criticisms are witty and his self-regard greatly exaggerated.

At the beginning of the chapter it was stated that Clark occasionally refers to his own 'heroic' accomplishments. His motivations for murder may not be readily apparent, but it can be assumed that he was a 'clean-up' killer. He clearly lacks remorse for victims of any sort. In a rambling letter about the victims who died in the World Trade Center on September 11 2001, he wrote:

All efforts on 9/11 were lethal to FDNY and civilians. Everything done killed more people than if you'd stood and watched. Stairwells were congested with fire crews lugging useless shit up, as civilians needed stairs to leave. What if some fucking clown with a bad comb over and lisp were to declare 'if you build this high you must try to establish evac systems' so at least some of the shrimps on the bar-bee can get below the fire. No one is real eager to say 'why didn't anyone use dozens of very proficient means to get those people above the fire, out? Run UP stairs??' What exactly were 100's of 'Polish cavalry' gonna do when they ran up onto the 'machine guns and artillery' of that huge 2200° + fire on 4–5 floors? Pee on it? Why was no fire-fighting box clamped under the big helo-cranes and flown up to fire water and slurry in the gaping holes, cooling the fire, making it burn at 1600° core? Why weren't stringers of 20–40 harnessed people pulled out of windows 10 stories, 20 stories above and around the building from the fire? No one wants to say that they were doomed from the start because NO ONE had decided every 20 stories should have rappel lines and accordion style tubes to allow 20 descents. It takes up an office, and offices rent for $50–$100 a square foot. Every square foot is worth a new jet-ski for some fat cat's kids, every year. I pass my time mentally exercising. I designed rough drafts of forest or high-rise fire/rescue birds, sea rescue choppers, and lots else. It's a mental torture; try it. Sorry, I do take my hobby seriously. To you it's a rant. I see it as railing against incompetent powers that be.

His explanation serves two purposes. First, it demonstrates that he has no tolerance for the struggles and accomplishments of others. Second, it reveals his tendency toward self-gratification. How could California possibly put such an indispensable mind to death? By proclaiming himself to be the person with all the right answers, he gives himself a necessary place in society. But he cannot disguise his contempt for others. Consider the following statement he gave in a letter dated 17 September 2002:

> Face it, mankind alone among successful species strives to help the least fit procreate the MOST. We assure diabetes will blossom as a 'disease' by assuring diabetics not only live long lives (fine), but wrecklessly procreate and 'pass on' the gene. The dumbest, laziest and least fit to survive without it, procreated like bunnies on the Great Society bullshit of the 60's–70's. I live with the first generation of that error. Evolution ceases when some species decides the least evolved and fit should spawn vastly higher than average numbers of young. Simple science, we are breeding the future into chaos.

Simply put, he appears to lack the capacity for empathy. He puts himself above everyone else and expects to be recognised as a 'genius'. If he has evolved beyond normal limits of humankind, then he considers it his right to decide who is least fit to survive. Simply substitute 'diabetics' with 'prostitutes' and you may have found the basis for his 'clean-up' justification of killing. He would never admit to it, however, as it is not the type of attention that he currently seeks. The attention he received from the murders has been replaced by the attention he attempts to get by playing the role of a victim of the justice system.

Along with contending that he is worthy of admiration, he also discredits and underestimates the accomplishments of others. Speaking to Detective Leroy Orozco, one of the officers who apprehended him, he said, 'Shouldn't you be home eating a taco?' His slurs are not only ethnic, as when speaking of one of the psychiatrists who evaluated him, he said, 'Gloria Keyes was an awesomely scared, "freaking out" nut case. She should NEVER be involved in criminal cases. She was scared of being scared. She used the MMPI diagnostic quiz and collected her exaggerated fee.' But Keyes' diagnosis was right on target, as she diagnosed him with Narcissistic Personality Disorder specified by grandiosity. Of course Clark took issue with her finding, saying:

> You either are a narcissist who is grandiose, or you are suffering low self-esteem and feel inferior to others. EVERYONE who knew me in '60–'80 said, are you nuts? Doug's a casual slob – narcissist? Ha! And even her 'support' for it was silly – 'he likes himself more than those (currently) trying to help him.' Shit, I knew what kind of bottom feeder she was – everyone knew it.

Even during his trial, Clark would bask in the attention afforded him by the media. He took an instant liking to Deputy District Attorney Robert Jorgensen's appearance and convinced a girlfriend to buy him a similar pin-striped suit. He even took a moment to pose for the press in his fashionable new attire. He was not impressed, however, with his court appointed defence attorneys. His first attorney, Karl Henry, was replaced by Paul Geragos. Because Clark insisted on serving as co-counsel, both attorneys found it impossible to represent him. He stubbornly refused to submit to their advice. Shortly thereafter, he was assigned Maxwell Keith. Keith would later receive a lifetime achievement award for his years of service, including his representation of a defendant in the Charles Manson murder trial. It should have been an impressive record to Clark, who had read everything that Manson prosecutor Vincent Bugliosi had ever written. By Bugliosi's own admission, Keith had been his most formidable opponent, from a group of more than a half-dozen defence attorneys who were involved in the Manson case. But this did not impress Clark, who insisted that he was his own best man for the occasion. He referred to Keith as a 'drunken asshole of a lawyer' and a 'useless court leach', whose conduct was 'so abysmally below par for legal conduct, it's got to be motivated by malice'.

Clark presented his own version of a defence. He claimed that Carol Bundy and her ex-boyfriend, Jack Murray, committed all the murders. His idea of a brilliant defence hinged on the name association between Carol Bundy and Ted Bundy. He insisted that the murders were committed as a copycat spree. It was so ridiculous that the court refused to hear it. Scorned by the justice system, he continues to present one appeal after another, using the copycat motive as his basis.

He apparently believed that Carol would go along with the idea, as he expected her to take the stand in his favour. As it turned out, she was the prosecution's star witness against him. She had finally taken enough of his abuse and demonstrated that she was no longer under his control. Furious that she refused to go along with his plans and still convinced he has a strong case, he said, 'Here's one that epitomizes her "blunt object to cranium" frustration with "stupid" adversaries in general – she doesn't respect ME, intellectually, either!' His apparent reason for why she killed Murray is that she wanted to get caught. He went on to explain, 'Her S/M lover is found stabbed 20+ times, head gone, pants to knees in a "homosexual rape" pose. Mutilated buttock, red panties on – she's *last to have been seen in murder vehicle with him.*'

In Douglas Clark's mind, the story is not over. His fragile ego will not allow him to accept responsibility for the Sunset Strip slayings. Believing himself superior to others, he did not expect to get caught. An unspoken truth is that he is intelligent enough to have made a productive contribution to society, but his own grandiosity became his undoing. It is this very same superiority complex that enables him to assert that he is not the killer. How could he have been caught by people so obviously inferior to him? The logical answer – he didn't get caught. He now has the monumental task of convincing the world that investigators caught the wrong guy. But no job is too big for a narcissist. In true cavalier form, he wrote to me, 'One day you'll see, I *guarantee* it!'

13. JOHN NORMAN COLLINS, THE CO-ED KILLER

It was the first day of spring, 1969. Scott was on his way to catch the school bus that would take him to Belleville Junior High. It was Friday, and his mind was lost among the possibilities of what might occupy his weekend. As he shuffled alongside the gated cemetery that stood beside his home, he absentmindedly stumbled upon a yellow raincoat. As he drew his attention to it, something jarred his consciousness. He was shocked to discover the disfigured body of a woman protruding from underneath the slicker. He ran home and told his mother. When the police arrived, they found what they believed to be the third victim in a series of brutal sex murders. For Scott, life would never be the same again. His bedroom window faced the gruesome site, and for the rest of his years in that house, he would refuse to sleep in his bedroom. Haunted by the image of the woman's battered face and bloated neck, he said that he feared he would one night look out and find her staring in.

Investigators could not be certain whether the victim was somehow linked to the others who were found several miles away. As the death toll continued to rise, they found little to correlate it with the tight geographic pattern that was developing. They did not know that the killer worked just down the road from where this victim was found. It is a fact that continues to evade notice, even today. The signature of mutilation was consistent, though it had been carried out to a lesser degree here than in most of the other cases. And this victim had been acquired from the same vicinity as the rest of them. The search for the Co-Ed Killer became the biggest manhunt in Michigan history. In addition to local and state authorities, the FBI was called in, as well as a noted international psychic.

John Norman did not always go by the last name of Collins. Born in Windsor, Canada in 1947, he never knew his father, who abandoned the family shortly after he was born, running off with another woman, never to be seen again by his wife and three children. John's mother, an attractive and superficial woman, quickly remarried. But little would be remembered of this marriage, as it lasted less than a year. Looking for a way to escape her misfortunes, she moved the family across the river to Detroit.

It was here that she met a man named Collins. He was an older man who had a stable job as an auto mechanic. He formally adopted the children, giving them his surname, along with naturalised US citizenship. But the relationship was soon fraught with episodic violence. Prone to jealous rages, their new stepfather often beat their mother. A chronic alcoholic, he turned the abuse towards them, as well. The relationship lasted little more than a couple of years. John was nine years old when the last of his failed father figures disappeared from his life.

Little is known of John's mother, but that is to be expected. Placing a great deal of emphasis on her stunning appearance, she had little difficulty attracting men; but maintaining relationships was another story. She was capable of establishing very intense connections with people, but the depth of these affiliations was always lacking. She was not physically or verbally abusive towards her children – if anything, she allowed them to get away with too much. For the most part, she paid little attention to them. But if they got into any type of trouble, she defended them vehemently. Children who are raised under such conditions often perceive this act of defending as an indication of their parents' protectiveness and affection. The need to feel loved is such a necessary component of human bonding that they seldom see the situation for what it truly is, an attempt by their parents to camouflage their own failures. And since it is a proven method of getting attention from their parents, often the only way to do so, they manufacture new conflicts without having to take any responsibility for them. Such children fail to recognise that their parents are acting out of regard for themselves.

Collins became a strikingly handsome young man. He was an honour student and star varsity athlete. In the classroom and on the field, he won the admiration of many teachers and fellow peers. Like his mother, he had little difficulty attracting attention from the opposite sex. But he would be remembered in other ways, as well.

Former girlfriends described him as intelligent and articulate, but angry most of the time. Little things seemed to set him off. He had no patience for people he regarded as ignorant. And if anyone did something to inadvertently offend him, he took it very personally. Astonishingly, it was his own sister who first experienced the brutality of his boiling rage.

She had become pregnant at the age of eighteen and was forced to marry. Collins had no special regard for her husband. But when he caught his sister with another man, he beat them both severely. Was it the act of infidelity that set him off, or did the beating reveal a deep-seated anger toward women he perceived as adulterous and untrustworthy?

Involvement with such women would surely bring to the surface his own feelings of vulnerability. If the women he was supposed to care most about in his life were capable of such transgressions, then were not all women dirty and unreliable? No man could straighten out a woman who was unfaithful. Even given his superior talents and abilities, women would always make him feel powerless and insecure. He did not wish to compromise his idyllic notion of the hierarchical structure of relationships. He was not to be disrespected by any woman, the object of both his fascination and contempt. If he wanted something, it was not for her to decline it.

He attended Eastern Michigan University in Ypsilanti. A blue collar town, it is known for its proximity to Ann Arbor, another university city, and several automotive manufacturing plants. It is few people's idea of an attractive setting, and those with the means to live elsewhere often do. But it is home to a well-respected teacher-education programme, and that is what Collins decided to pursue. After a year at Central Michigan University, he had decided to become an elementary teacher. The transfer brought him closer to home. Even so, he seldom visited his family. An aunt lived nearby. Her husband was a state trooper, who had been assigned to the Ypsilanti post. Collins would spend more time visiting his aunt and uncle than his own mother or siblings.

It was about this time that his aunt, his mother's younger sister, noticed a startling change in his attitude. The once witty boy had become a cynical and unforgiving young man. He did not take kindly to suggestions that he should visit his mother. She was now seeing a wealthy man from St Clair, and he was aware that this man had been assisting his mother with payment of his own college tuition. But something had happened to strain the relationship between mother and son. Perhaps it was not a single event, but rather a constellation of things. After all, his older brother and sister had also abandoned their mother. His sister may have moved in with her, but it became obvious that she only pursued the arrangement so that she could have a babysitter, someone else to be responsible for the infant, while she went about her own selfish and carefree way. It seemed the Collins children had learned the lessons of their mother.

John Collins had done well during his first few semesters at college. He demonstrated a keen intellect and instinct for the proper education of school-aged children. He had been a top student himself in the elementary grades, and as a child, school had provided the one stable environment in which he could control the outcome of his efforts by achieving recognition for outstanding marks. But towards the end of his degree programme, his performance had taken a turn for the worse. As intelligent as he was, it would have to be assumed that this was due to his own decision to pursue other avenues.

He was interested in motorcycles, and a great deal of his time was spent tinkering with these fascinating machines. Smart enough to earn a comfortable living that would enable him to purchase several motorcycles for himself, and clever enough to figure out ways to avoid working for them, he began stealing various parts from different models to build his own customised machines. His love of motorcycles would later indirectly help to implicate him in the disappearance of his last known victim.

His first victim was nineteen-year-old Mary Fleszar. A petite and studious young woman, she was neither the careless nor seductive type that matches the stereotypical profile of a victim. She was not much of a risk taker. A gifted student at Eastern, she had landed a four-year academic scholarship to study accounting. She was last seen walking towards her apartment just before 9.00 p.m. on 9 July 1967, when a man sitting on his front porch observed a car pull up alongside her. She evidently did not know the driver, as she declined the offer of a ride. The car sped around the corner and came back up the block. This time, it pulled directly in front of her. The driver was a persistent young man, but Fleszar possessed too great a share of common sense to get in with him. Circling around behind the car, she crossed the street and headed towards her apartment. The orange-coloured polka-dot tent dress was the last image seen by the witness, as Fleszar disappeared beyond the glow of an overhead street lamp.

When they found her, a month had already passed. Two boys aged fifteen were preparing to plough a field near the corner of Geddes and LaForge roads when they heard a car door slam. Anxious to see if they could catch a pair of young lovers in what was known to be a favourite make-out spot, they quietly made their way towards the abandoned structure that had once been a farmhouse on the property. The weeds were tall, so getting there undetected would not be a problem. But just as they were about to part the overgrowth, the car sped away. The boys entered the clearing. A set of tyre tracks angled off the driveway, pointing in an odd direction and making them curious. Following the path through tall weeds, they noticed a foul stench. As they came upon the source of it, they found a misshapen carcass lying amidst a pile of litter. It was black and leathery, and had been dead a long time. It was nearly impossible to make out what it had once been, until one of the boys noticed that it appeared to have a human ear.

When the medical examiner arrived, several disturbing observations were made. First, the body was not completely intact. Half of one arm was missing, as were the fingers of the opposite hand. Both feet had also been severed. Animals had got to it, as bite marks were present on the skin and exposed bones. Insects had also nested, and the state of decomposition was accelerated by their burrowing. But a qualified examiner can determine several things from a victim's presentation. This one had been dead for about a month, and the body had been moved to this location from elsewhere. Moreover, someone had visited the site several times, and had moved it on each occasion. Although the exact cause of death would be difficult to establish, it was clearly a homicide. The victim had been stabbed in the chest repeatedly. The body also appeared to have been brutally beaten.

Crime scene investigators uncovered a pile of clothing beneath a scrap of corrugated metal sheeting. Among the clothes was an orange-coloured dress with white polka dots. It had been slashed down the front, and the victim's brassière and panties were also in the pile. They, too, had been partially torn. An oral surgeon matched the victim's dental structure to a chart provided by a local dentist. The results confirmed what everyone had already suspected. Less than three miles from where she had been abducted, the body of Mary Fleszar had been found.

The killer's fascination with his handiwork had brought him back to the dump site time and again. But it did not stop there. Prior to the funeral, a handsome young man arrived at the funeral home claiming to be a friend of the victim's family. He asked to take a picture of the body. He was refused permission, but it was not until he left that the attendant realised that the visitor had not even been in possession of a camera. Speculation arose that this was the killer. He was apparently infatuated with the macabre object of his creation. Unfortunately, no one could provide a detailed description of the visitor and he would be free to prowl again, searching for a replacement to satisfy his autoerotic urges.

Collins continued to exhibit little difficulty in meeting and dating new women. In fact, he possessed such a degree of confidence that he often came across as cocky and arrogant. Approaching women on the street, he would invite them to take a ride with him. Even if he was unknown to many of these women, it was likely that they may have seen him before. Eastern's campus is not all that big: at the time, it had an enrolment of only 13,000 students. Anyone with a great deal of mobility could easily become a familiar sight. And he was outgoing. Could he have been the young man who had attempted to get Fleszar into a car that night? If so, what was his motivation for pursuing her?

As it turns out, they were probably familiar with one another. He had worked across the hall from the Field Services Office, where she held a part-time job on campus. And unknown to everyone else at the time, she had recently sought medical attention for a suspected pregnancy. She had told medical staff that she had been raped by a classmate after offering him a ride across campus. There was reason to believe that she had received an abortion just prior to her disappearance. Collins was known to be sexually aggressive, and he had dealt punishing blows in the past. Perhaps his anger had got the best of him and he had lashed out at the person who had scorned him. Given his vocational ambitions to teach at elementary school and his own unresolved issues of childhood neglect, he was unlikely to be very understanding of any woman's decision to exercise control over an unborn child. Such single-minded-ness could also account for his unmitigated rage towards all women, who possessed the power to give life and take it away.

If women were considered the embodiment of all that was evil and unclean, it would not take long before he demonstrated these feelings in a comment made to a young woman he was dating. After beginning to kiss and fondle her, he suddenly stopped and asked if she was menstruating. When she answered affirmatively, he angrily pushed her away with the comment, 'That is really disgusting!' Whether he was angry that he would not be able to have sex with her or truly felt an aversion to a woman's cycle, he became childlike in his reaction to the situation and promptly stormed off.

And something else was noted of his behaviour. At about the time of Fleszar's disappearance, he had stopped attending classes. With only 24 credit hours remaining to complete his degree, he had given up his goal of becoming a teacher. The problems of childhood were unfair, but he was powerless to do anything about it. Ultimately, it was a woman's world. If women were in control of a child's psychological development, and if it was their job to ensure that a child received the proper care and attention, then it was pointless for him to play that role. And yet they were stupid for not recognising how important it was to provide these things. He could level the playing field by exercising control over them. There were plenty of ways to get his revenge.

Joan Schell was a twenty-year-old art student. Although news of the Fleszar murder had shocked residents of Ypsilanti and the surrounding area, almost a year had passed since the incident occurred. It was 30 June, and Joan had just returned to her apartment from a weekend visit to her parents in Plymouth. They had dropped her off at 9.15 p.m. Shortly thereafter, she made arrangements to meet her boyfriend in Ann Arbor. She could take the Short Way Line, a bus service that followed a routine schedule between the neighbouring cities. Arriving on time for the final 10.30 run, she waited 45 minutes. The bus never came. Her room-mate, who had gone along to keep her company at the bus stop, suggested that they return to their apartment. But Joan was more determined than ever that she would get to Ann Arbor.

A car slowed in front of them, but did not stop. Three young men were inside, and they appeared to take an interest in the room-mates. This was confirmed when the car came back around the block, and this time stopped. A good-looking young man stepped out. Judging by the green EMU T-shirt, he was probably a fellow student. He asked if they needed a ride. Joan explained that she was trying to get to Ann Arbor. Easing her room-mate's quiet objection, she promised to phone her when she arrived at her destination. The call never came.

Collins was clearly the ladies' man of the trio. He suggested that they return to his apartment, where he could give her a lift in his own car. It turned out that he lived just across the street from her. Since they were neighbours, it did not seem like a very risky proposition. He did not return home until after 2.00 a.m. In his possession was her red purse. He explained that she had left it in his car.

Five days later, her body was discovered by a road-construction crew. Her throat had been slashed and she had been stabbed in the chest at least five times. Her miniskirt was twisted cruelly around her neck. Judging by the state of decomposition about the face and upper torso, she had been dead several days. But from the waist down, the corpse appeared fresh. It was not difficult to determine that she had been sexually penetrated, and it was soon obvious that she had not been killed there. In fact, she had only recently been dumped at the site. Whoever had done this had somehow managed to preserve her lower body, and had possibly continued to use it for purposes of sexual arousal and gratification after her death. But how had this been done, and who could have orchestrated such a disturbing atrocity?

Authorities had little to go on, but Collins soon educated his room-mates about the graphic details of the murder. Should they suspect that he was somehow involved, however, he had a ready explanation for why he knew so much about it. His uncle was a corporal with the state police, and had given him a detailed analysis of the crime scene. This was good enough for his friends, but it would not convince a jury. Later on, it would be learned that Collins knew more than could possibly have been known by his uncle. Meanwhile, Schell's boyfriend had become the primary suspect in the case.

He was AWOL from the army, and that did little to avert suspicion. But with eyewitness accounts from Schell's room-mate and a girl who lived in the vicinity in which the pick-up occurred, it was difficult to establish how a chance encounter with three young men could somehow be connected with the boyfriend, who had been anxiously awaiting her arrival in Ann Arbor. The boyfriend was cleared, but police still had no solid information on the identity of the killer. It would be more than eight months before another body turned up.

This time it would be 23-year-old Jane Mixer. She was a first-year law student at the University of Michigan, in neighbouring Ann Arbor. In what was becoming a familiar story, she had agreed to take a ride with someone she did not know. But this was different; it was not spontaneous. Jane had accepted her boyfriend's marriage proposal, and had made arrangements for a ride home to announce the engagement to her family. Since she did not own a car, she had posted a notice on the message board in the student union, hoping to catch a ride with someone who might be heading the two-and-a-half-hour drive toward Muskegon. She had felt lucky to have been able to solicit a response so quickly, and had jotted the caller's name on a scrap of paper. The words 'David Johnson' and '6.30' were the only clues to his identity.

Her battered body was found lying at the entrance to a cemetery in Denton Township, less than a few miles from the outskirts of Ypsilanti. It was a grisly discovery for the thirteen-year-old boy who was on his way to catch the school bus. Medical examiners concluded that she had been killed by two bullets from a .22-caliber gun, both of which had entered her head. And as was characteristic of one of the earlier slayings, she was found with an article of clothing twisted around her neck. In this case, the stocking had been stretched so tightly that it was buried deep within the bloated flesh. Her skirt had been pulled up above the waist, and her panties had been pulled down. A sanitary pad was still in place, which seemed to indicate that she had not been sexually penetrated. But the crime itself was clearly sexual in nature.

Sexual predators do not always commit their offences the same way each time. As they become more sophisticated, they refine their approach. They are oriented towards a single purpose and goal – to incorporate fantasy into reality. To do so, they must author a fantasy-driven reality. This requires planning and a singularity of purpose. All actions have meaning, and any action that is outside the scope of their purpose is a wasted action. Therefore, only actions that are relevant are committed; extraneous motions are eliminated.

Such appears to have been the case in the Mixer homicide. This was Collins's third known murder, and the victim had been acquired through premeditated planning. Rather than seeking a chance encounter, he manipulated a set of circumstances to arrive at a situation in which he was in control of all the variables. Taking her telephone number from the student union bulletin board, he phoned her with an assumed identity. The identity, it was later discovered, had been taken from a man who belonged to a fraternity where Collins had once been a member. The level of planning was sophisticated. Such sophistication is not uncommon for serial killers, who become more adept at authoring their fantasies after the first couple of kills. And there are indications that he was following the news of his crimes very carefully, as well as being keen to maximise their impact in the media. Although the first couple of victims had been placed in slightly more remote locations than the others, they were not far from the beaten path. In fact, they had been intentionally placed for easy discovery. The third victim was given the most obvious placement of all. As he had taken such a bold risk this time, it is understandable that the body did not exhibit the same degree of post-mortem degradation as the others, although it did receive the characteristic savage garroting by a stocking after death.

And then there were other coincidences. Collins had worked night-shifts at the Motor Wheel Plant, located just up the road from this latest dump site. And months later, a search of his residence would yield a box of .22-caliber shells, indicating that he had access to the same type of firearm that had been used in the murder. If he had promised Mixer a ride to Muskegon, the fastest route would have taken them right through Denton Township, where the cemetery is clearly visible from US-12. Moreover, the area includes several seldom-travelled side roads, most of which are hidden from direct view. He would undoubtedly have been familiar with them, as most of them led off the road he took to and from work. It is little coincidence that one of them happened to be an unpaved and isolated section of Geddes Road, on the better known part of which he had deposited the body of Mary Fleszar.

Attention was frenzied in the press. While police were chasing the false lead of 'David Johnson' that they had located in a search of Mixer's apartment, the killer was hard at work. Just four days after the discovery of the third victim, a fourth one was found less than a quarter of a mile away from where the second one had been discovered by construction workers the previous summer. The killer was clearly drawn to the attention he was receiving, and he had decided to up the ante. His deliberate attempts to toy with police would become a trademark of each new crime. They were also a clear demonstration of his growing confidence and cunning.

Maralynn Skelton was only sixteen years old. But despite her chronological age, she was well attuned to the candid ways of the world. The problem was that she was smarter than most of her peers. She was bored with the condescending power structure of the typical classroom, so she decided to drop out of school. With an IQ of 123, she could manage her way through life by taking all the shortcuts. Money was not too difficult to come by. She only needed to expand her contacts with a sympathetic college market, and the distribution of drugs would keep her afloat. But through these activities she would encounter numerous situations of significant risk. She had developed a pretty good radar for assessing danger, but she walked among an unpredictable crowd. It would take a very convincing stranger to lower her guard.

As it turned out, she was preoccupied with trying to track down her boyfriend. He did not know that she had returned to town, after she had left with her family to a new home in Flint. No one had bothered to get her opinion before deciding to move, so she sought to express it by making her way back to Ann Arbor. She called around when she got there, but no one had seen her boyfriend. She phoned a friend in Ypsilanti, who told her to come on over. Hitching a ride from the Arborland shopping centre to Eastern Michigan University should not have been a problem; it was little more than three miles from one point to the next. But Maralynn did not make it to her intended destination.

Instead, she turned up in a construction site, where a new subdivision was being built just around the corner from Geddes Road. She had been so violently assaulted that the degree of overkill was nauseating. Her skull had been shattered into large fragments, and vicious welts covered her torso and upper legs. A garter belt had been wrapped around her neck, and a wad of dark-blue cloth had been jammed down her windpipe. The rough limb of a tree branch had been shoved eight inches into her vagina. But what made the scene even more disturbing was the report by the medical examiner. According to the nature of the wounds and strap marks found across her breasts, she had been alive but immobilised during most of the assault. The killer was escalating his degree of violence, but he was still careful not to give anything up. His dump sites were becoming more public, but investigators could not determine where any of the murders had taken place.

The cycle had accelerated. Between victims three and four, the cooling off period lasted only three days. Possible explanations might include the gratifying attention from the media, or a sense of unfinished business with the third victim. Hers was a high-profile abduction, and the killer had disposed of her body almost immediately. He may have been concerned that authorities could trace her last known steps more carefully than in his previous murders, and that these might somehow lead to his identity. After all, he had set the abduction up with considerable forethought. What if Mixer had talked to someone about the man she was supposed to meet? In retrospect, it had been stupid of him to describe the car to her, but how else was she supposed to recognise who was coming to pick her up? She had talked about a fiancé as they made their way out of Ann Arbor, and her family knew that she was on the way home for a visit. What if she had told one of them about the car she would be riding in? The more he thought about it, the less far-fetched it seemed. And if it was just an overreaction on his part, he reminded himself that nothing could be left to chance. Perhaps another victim would divert attention from the last one.

The gruesome discovery of 25 March had done just that. But keeping a low profile would be hard to do. Like most killers, he liked to talk about his crimes. He did not identify himself, of course, but he was obsessed with talking about the murders. He explained to friends and room-mates that the bodies had been displayed for easy discovery, so that the killer could get recognition for his crimes. Any good forensic psychologist would know that. But he also demonstrated something that went beyond sound psychological observation when he insisted that the victims had deserved to die. This lack of empathy was disturbing to his friends, and it would become much more so once he was implicated in the murders.

Despite his intelligence, Collins was an egoist. He did not subscribe to the common view of moral ethics. In a highly philosophical English paper, he had written, 'If a person wants something, he alone is the deciding factor of whether or not to take it, regardless of what society thinks may be right or wrong. If a person holds a gun on somebody, it's up to him to decide whether to take the other's life or not. The point is: It's not society's judgment that's important, but the individual's own choice of will and intellect.' If killing was a purely intellectual act that could be considered without the complications of emotion, then morality could be objectified and then removed from the equation. Respect for human life would be immaterial. To prove his point, he once told a girlfriend that if it was right for a man to kill, then he had to do it. Further explaining his position, he said that the perfect crime was committed without guilt. Guilt, he insisted, was how people got caught.

But philosophy and science do not always agree. The murderer who committed these crimes was cautious, but the narcissist who delighted in their attention was not. He made a suspect of himself to at least one other person. On a drive through a wooded area, he pulled alongside the road and asked her if she would be scared to find out that he was the Co-Ed Killer. He explained that being alone with him could be dangerous, if he decided to make her the next victim. But she did not believe that he was the killer. It simply made no sense that the real killer would identify himself so casually. She was lucky. The next person to take a ride with him would not be so fortunate.

Dawn Basom disappeared on 15 April. She was a cautious thirteen-year-old from Ypsilanti. Possessed of a good mind, she would never have taken a ride with a stranger. She was walking home from a friend's house just before dusk. Her route took her along a set of railroad tracks, where she encountered a couple of boys she knew, fishing from a small footbridge over the Huron River. She stopped to talk to them for a couple of minutes, then, observing the fading sunset, she asked if they would escort her the remaining distance to her home. The boys declined, telling her that they also had to leave, and that their homes were in the opposite direction. It was a refusal that would haunt them for the rest of their lives. As Dawn made her way from the tracks, less than a half-mile from her home, she vanished without a trace.

Her mother had been a worried widow for the past six years. Recognising the frailty of life, she had instilled in her youngest child the importance of a cautious sensibility. And yet Dawn had not come home. After making several concerned calls to each of Dawn's friends, she phoned the police. Sensing that this was not a girl who would do something irresponsible such as run away, they took down her description. Because of this, there was little doubt about the identity of the girl who would later be found dead on the side of Gale Road. Only twelve hours had passed since the time of her disappearance, and this time the killer had left an unexpected clue.

The body had been left in plain view, and a motorist passing through the area noticed it right away. She had been strangled with black electrical wire and stabbed repeatedly in the chest. Like the others, her body was left in a semi-nude pose. Only her brassière and blouse were present, and they had been lifted to expose deep slashes across both breasts. The medical examiner would also discover a torn piece of her blouse that had been shoved into the back of her throat. It was evident that she had been killed elsewhere, but the location could not be too far away.

The sheriff quickly organised a search party, which fanned out in all possible directions from the scene of her discovery. The shoes were found first, having probably been tossed from a moving vehicle as it made its way towards the dump site. Strangely enough, they appeared to have particles of broken glass embedded into each sole. Concentrating on the direction from which the killer must have travelled, they soon came upon an abandoned farmhouse. Basom's orange-coloured mohair sweater was found just outside the structure, only a few feet from the rear of the deserted dwelling. A search of the premises revealed several clues. The stairs to the basement were littered with fragments of broken glass, which matched the particles found in the soles of the shoes. A piece of the victim's blouse was discovered in the corner of the basement, as were several traces of fresh blood. And a search of the barn turned up a coil of black electrical wire, which exactly matched the piece that had been embedded in her throat. The murder site had been discovered! And with its discovery, perhaps another question had been answered. One of the windows allowed a certain amount of sunlight to penetrate its dank interior. If the body of Joan Schell had been taken to this basement, then it might explain how the lower part of her body had remained somewhat preserved. If the upper part of her body had been exposed to the sunlight that pierced this sombre torture chamber, then it would have decayed more rapidly. What might this say about the killer's attempt to depersonalise his victims? Whatever the killer's philosophy and motivation, the patient persistence of science was not on his side.

The authorities did not believe that Basom had gone willingly with her abductor. In fact, they speculated that he had pulled a gun. Most serial killers are unassuming and reassuring. They are masterful at gaining a person's trust. But when that does not work, they can always resort to a back-up plan. She was most likely to have been taken by force. But what connection did the killer have with this particular neighbourhood? Although it bordered on Eastern's campus, it was a blue-collar community that seemed to have little in common with the campus atmosphere. Only later would it be discovered that Collins was familiar with the area, as he had once dated a girl who lived in the apartment complex located on the very same street as Basom's house. The authorities were still no closer to the identity of the killer, but a chain of circumstantial evidence was growing that would one day convict the man responsible for the slayings.

Police were hopeful that the killer would return to the murder site. They decided to stake out the deserted farmhouse. During a routine round of inspection, one of the officers made a startling discovery. The killer had in fact returned. He had somehow entered the premises unseen, but he had certainly come back to the basement where Dawn Basom was murdered. Much to everyone's surprise, he had left a gold-plated earring and a piece of white cloth in plain view of anyone making the rounds. The earring had belonged to Maralynn Skelton, and the piece of cloth had been taken from the blouse of Dawn Basom. It was obvious – the killer was basking in the notoriety. He must have believed himself superior to the police, for now he would enjoy playing games with them.

Less than two months would pass before another victim was taken. Alice Kalom was a 23-year-old graduate student in the fine arts programme at the University of Michigan. She was last known to be seen on 7 June, at a popular dance club called the Depot House. Was it possible that the killer had been actively prowling for another victim, choosing to cruise a location where he could take his pick of the scene?

He had been conspicuously quiet for several weeks. For one thing, he knew that his favoured execution site was under surveillance. It was the closest they had come to catching him. Much of the community was moreover under a heightened state of alert, with the media coverage remaining steady. At this point, he was as concerned with his public image as he was with self-preservation. He would kill again, this much he knew, but the message to be delivered in the interim was that they were dealing with somebody larger than themselves. He would not get caught, because no one *could* catch him. He was unstopp-able. He could convince himself of this by demonstrating superiority over those who were assigned to stop him. For the men in uniform, it was just a job; but for him, it was his life's chosen work. To prove the point, he had penetrated their barrier and left a calling card. But should they forget who was calling the shots, he could take back what little they thought they had. They were far too smug in their imagined possession of the crime scene. After all, it belonged to him. The only significant thing to have ever happened there was by his own design. And so three-and-a-half weeks before the next victim was to be taken, the entire place went up in flames.

The media is a powerful apparition. Its spectre loomed over everything that developed in the story. It reported facts, but also attempted to prescribe the popular point of view. As a tool, it proved invaluable to the killer. He could practically author his own headlines, and it was very gratifying to see his handiwork in print. But for the public, it was a dangerous business indeed. Sure, the headlines would inform them of the need to be careful, but it also informed them of the killer's success. A new dynamic now played into his deadly cycle of power portrayal, as he was goaded on by the attention. As such, the next victim would be taken from a very public and ostensibly safe place.

The Depot House was a popular nightclub that had once been a train station. A local band was scheduled to perform that evening, and a large crowd was expected. Alice Kalom had been invited to attend by the band's front man, but it is unlikely that she ever made it to the performance. Although several acquaint-ances reported seeing her there, none of them had actually spoken to her. And it was later learned, much to the investigators' chagrin, that several closer friends had noticed a woman who bore a slight resemblance to her there. Nonethe-less, the papers had reported her last known whereabouts as the party at the Depot House. It was a false lead that cost the authorities a precious amount of expeditious time.

They were unable to either determine her last known movements or locate a crime scene. They found her body but, as with all the others, she had been mutilated elsewhere. The cause of death was strikingly similar to that of Jane Mixer. Both had been killed by a .22-caliber bullet to the head. They had also sustained savage injuries to the throat, the most recent victim's being slashed from ear to ear. Investigators also found multiple stab wounds to her chest, two of which had punctured the heart. And just like all the others, her panties had been torn away. In this case, a pair of panty hose was also present, the crotch slashed down the middle. Investigators may have harboured some doubt concerning the serial killer's responsibility for Mixer's death, but he was undoubtedly responsible for this one. Not only was she discovered on the lot of an abandoned farmhouse, but the location was only a few miles north from where they had found the bodies of Schell and Skelton.

What, if anything, did the victims have in common with one another? So far, they all seemed to have long brown or reddish-brown hair, but that was common among the majority of women in the area, so it did not seem to provide much to go on. Most had been wearing a dress or type of skirt, but that also seemed common enough. In short, they could find very little that resembled a pattern, outside of the obvious pattern of modus operandi. Would a psychological profile be helpful? The killer had confidence. He had been able to pick up his victims without any sign of struggle. He could apparently approach them with little risk of raising alarm. And once he had them, ending their lives was easy. But perhaps he was not as confident as was suggested at first glance. The two oldest victims, Jane Mixer and Alice Kalom, had been murdered with a gun. Was he a person who felt more comfortable and in control with younger females? Did he find the older ones a bit more intimidating? Clearly possessed of some form of stereotypical victim selection, the next thing to be determined was whether or not he had been personally familiar with any of them.

It turned out that Collins did know Kalom. She had recently completed a degree in architecture and design and was pursuing a teaching certificate at about the same time that he would have been seeking his teaching internship. But that might have been mere coincidence. Yet she had somehow come willingly to his apartment that day. As reported by his room-mate, Collins had given her a ride to the apartment on the back of his motorcycle. Shortly after their arrival, an argument took place in the bedroom, and she ran out. He chased after her as she made her way onto the street, and he returned later without her. When her body was discovered the following day, the print of a boot was found on the white skirt. It would later be matched to a pair worn by Collins.

Physical evidence was being accumulated at a rapid pace, but law enforcement would have to wait until a suspect was found before any of it would prove useful. At this point, an arrest did not seem imminent. The community was in a state of panicked fear. And some of it was turning to outrage. How could the authorities have missed the killer, when it was reported that he had come back to the very site of one of his murders? A citizens group decided to take action. Known as the Psychedelic Rangers, they enlisted the help of one of the world's best-known psychics.

Peter Hurkos had fallen from a ladder nearly thirty years before the co-ed murders took place. He survived the four-story fall from the house he was painting, but was never quite the same afterwards. He started to 'know things' about people that they had never told anyone else. More importantly, he discovered that he could frequently visualise when something was about to happen to someone. At first, it was disturbing. Was it a gift or a curse to know so much about what was going to happen to people, especially when so many bad things often occurred? But if it was his lot to suffer such knowledge, why not use it? He accepted the Rangers' invitation to hunt for the Co-Ed Killer.

The police received him with little enthusiasm. After all, he had been called upon to assist with something that they had been unable to solve. But it did not take long before a few of the officers were impressed by his abilities. He could determine little from the previous murders, but he did have quite a bit to say about what they would find with the next one.

He predicted that the next victim would be found with a badly beaten face, and that the body would be discovered in a wooded ravine. When asked where, he said the location was called 'Riverview' or 'River Drive'. When asked to describe the killer, he provided several accurate details. Among them, he explained that the killer was a student who drove a motorcycle, and that he was slightly built with an attractive face. Among the details that seemed most ambiguous, he said that the man occasionally wore a moustache and was somehow associated with a ladder. Collins was not known to wear a moustache. At the time, he did not have one, although today he does. As for the ladder, not only would it be used in the commission of his final murder, but it was also the object that instigated a chain of seemingly unimportant observations which led to his discovery.

The psychic's legendary reputation had not gone unnoticed by Collins. Two days after his arrival, a phone call warned him to leave or consider himself responsible for the next murder. In a clandestine attempt to match wits with the unwitting psychic, Collins fearfully entered a restaurant where Hurkos was giving a presentation. It was a bold move, but he was desperate to make sure that the man could not identify him. Afterwards, he told friends that Hurkos was a fraud. The question on their minds should have been, 'How did he know?'

At the time of Hurkos's arrival, Collins had just returned from a brief trip to California. The significance of this trip would be revealed in another of the psychic's statements. Sensing that the authorities were not certain that the same killer had committed all six murders, he articulated and responded to this uncertainty with an adamant insistence that the same person was responsible, and intimated that other murders had also taken place at the hands of this killer. This would later be confirmed when police ran a check on an unsolved homicide that had taken place nearly two years earlier, in an area several miles south of Ypsilanti. But that was not all that Hurkos had been talking about. The most recent murder had not been connected to the killer because the body had been discovered in California!

Collins and a friend named Andrew Manuel worked the night-shift together at the Motor Wheel Plant on Ecorse Road. Their association was built on a common practice of stealing automotive parts for their various collected vehicles. Both considered themselves to be fairly talented backyard mechanics, and Collins was always in the market for new parts to keep his motorcycles running. Following a series of local break-ins, in which Collins had acquired the .22-caliber high-standard revolver that had probably been used in some of his slayings, the two of them decided on a much grander scheme of felony theft. They would steal a camper and take it with them to Manuel's native state of California. It was here that Collins met Roxie Phillips, an attractive seventeen-year-old girl who was on her way to mail a letter when she disappeared on the afternoon of 30 June.

Her body was found on 13 July in Pescadero Canyon. Two boys had been out hunting for fossils when they discovered it. The body was in an advanced state of decomposition. It was nude, except for a pair of sandals and a red-and-white-coloured belt that was embedded securely around the neck. The corpse had been deposited among a stand of poison oak, and there were indications that it had been carried there from elsewhere. A friend of the victim's would recall that she and Roxie had met a man named John, and that he had claimed to be a senior in college who was studying to become a teacher. In addition, he was visiting from Michigan, and had been staying in a camper with a friend. Each coincidence was too close to be considered mere chance.

Collins had moreover been treated at a nearby medical centre for what was diagnosed as a reaction to poison oak. Manuel knew nothing of the abduction and subsequent murder, as would later be revealed through a series of polygraph examinations given by the FBI. But he could account for Collins's whereabouts. The two of them had gone to Carmel, California in a camper that had been purchased with a bad cheque. Collins had left his sight for a short period of time, sometime during the afternoon of 30 June.

Some time later in Michigan, a search of Collins's car would yield a piece of red and white cloth that exactly matched the belt which was found around the victim's neck. But he would not be tied to this murder just yet. It was to be another victim that would prove his undoing. And the brutality of this murder demonstrated a brazen contempt for the law and all who dared to challenge him.

Karen Sue Beineman was a vivacious eighteen-year-old freshman, who had persuaded her parents to allow her to attend early courses at Eastern during the summer. News of the slayings was fresh in everyone's minds, but Karen was a sensible young woman. She had never tried drugs or alcohol, and she was possessed of a healthy mind and spirit. Furthermore, she agreed to live in a 'girls only' residence hall. Surely, if something had happened to those other girls, it must have been because they had not taken all the necessary precautions. And so she began her first term at Eastern, planning to earn a degree in special education.

On Wednesday 23 July, she was anticipating a visit from her boyfriend. The two of them had been dating for more than a year. They did not get to see much of one another because he was graduating college at the time she was finishing high school, but the future looked promising. Both of them planned to pursue careers in teaching. In preparation for his visit, she walked to a shop on Washington Street, where she intended to pick up some hair extensions that she had been waiting for.

Along the way, she dropped a letter in the mailbox. It was a friendly letter to her parents, thanking them for allowing her to come early to Eastern. She also included a front-page clipping of the co-ed murder investigations, across the top of which she had written, 'Don't worry folks. I am being careful.'

Collins was riding his Triumph motorcycle that day. He tried unsuccessfully to pick up a girl he noticed walking from campus towards an office supply shop on Washington Street. He offered her a ride, but she declined. He was persistent, she later remembered, but not rude or discourteous. Failing to make the right impression, he drove off. Perhaps he would have better luck with the next one.

Beineman was just up the street when he spotted her. A pretty girl with brown-coloured hair, she seemed a promising prospect. Stopping alongside her, he asked if she would accept a ride to wherever she was going. She was hesitant. Collins explained that it would be the safest thing to do, considering all the recent murders of girls who had been out walking alone. She replied that it would not be necessary, since she had just about reached her intended destination, and thanked him for the offer. He answered that it was no problem, and asked if she would mind if he followed along, just to make sure that she got there safely. She didn't mind. What was she supposed to do, tell him that he couldn't ride his bike on a public street? Besides, he was very charming and good-looking. A clean-cut young man like him was nothing to be concerned about. He was just a friendly student who seemed to have some kind of interest in her. It was a harmless favour. After picking up the wiglet, she went outside and climbed on the motorcycle with him.

She was found in a ditch along Riverside Drive, located near Huron River Drive in Ann Arbor. An elderly couple was out walking that afternoon when they came upon the startling discovery. She had been strangled and beaten. Her misshapen face told part of the story. She had been beaten with such obscene force that one eye was swollen completely shut and her bloodstained lips had swelled to conceal a shattered set of teeth. Revolting burns scorched her breasts, and it was evident that they had been caused by a corrosive liquid that had been poured down her neck and shoulders. The flesh was so badly damaged that deep layers of skin had peeled away. Ligature marks were present around each wrist, indicating that she had been tied and possibly suspended from something overhead. A piece of burlap cloth was found lodged in her throat, and her panties had been shoved deep inside her vagina.

From the description provided by employees at the wig shop, the suspect was a clean-cut young man with dark hair, who had given the customer a ride on his motorcycle. Since most motorcyclists did not fit that exact description, the pool of potential suspects could be narrowed significantly. An official canvass of the area pointed to several possibilities, among them Collins. But the rookie officer who questioned him gave too much away about what they were looking for, and Collins quickly provided an alibi. He told the officer that he had been to his aunt and uncle's house to feed their dog while they were away on vacation. The officer thanked him for his time, then left. Immediately afterwards, Collins retrieved a box of the victims' personal effects. A room-mate noticed him removing the box from their apartment, and Collins explained to him that the items had been stolen from various women, and that he did not wish to be booked on possession of stolen property. The room-mate had no reason to suspect that the articles belonged to the murdered women, and Collins was not about to tell him.

Corporal Dan Leik of the Ypsilanti post of the State Police could not believe that his nephew had been questioned in connection with the murders. Leik had just returned home from vacation with his wife and three young children when Collins told him about the inquiry. Obviously it was all a misunderstanding. He would see what he could find out as soon as he returned to work. Collins thanked his uncle and went on his way. Meanwhile, Leik went down to the basement to tell his wife the astonishing news. She was busy washing clothes, but not too preoccupied to notice that a few things were out of place.

She asked her husband what he had been doing with the ladder. Nothing, he answered. So why, then, had it been moved from its usual place? It was in the way of the washing machine. He answered that John must have moved it. Of course – John had been watching the house while they were away. But there was something else. He noticed several dark circles of paint that had been sprayed deliberately over the cement surface of the floor. Something was awry.

He phoned a couple of guys from the crime lab. They arrived to begin analysis of the paint and any substances that might be found beneath it. After scraping several spots, they determined that the disguised substance was nothing more than varnish. Why, then, would their nephew have sprayed paint over the top of a few old drops of varnish? It still did not make any sense. But then Leik asked them to scrape a section partially obscured by the edge of the washing machine. It revealed traces of human blood!

Forensics took a closer look at the basement. A section of one of the overhead pipes was found to be free of the dusty build-up that clung to all the other sections. It was likely that something had recently been suspended from this location. Several clippings of hair were also found beneath the washer. It was not an unusual find in itself, as Collins's aunt had often clipped her children's hair in the basement, but it was very significant in light of the clippings that had been discovered in the victim's panties, once they had been removed from her vaginal canal.

Collins was tried and convicted on overwhelming circumstantial evidence. Much physical evidence was also uncovered. In a search of his apartment, police found a necklace made from a 1967 Canadian silver dollar (which had belonged to the first victim, Mary Fleszar), a hunting knife that was consistent with the stab wounds found on several of his victims, and a box of

.22-caliber ammunition. Even so, Collins proclaimed his innocence.

He is serving a life sentence in Michigan's Marquette Branch Prison, a maximum security facility that houses the state's most violent offenders. He is not eligible for parole, though he continues to appeal the decision. Should he ever succeed, two other states might take an interest in charging him with murder. California could request to try him for the murder of Roxie Phillips, and Ohio, another death-penalty state, could seek charges for the disappearance of thirteen-year-old Eileen Adams. She was kidnapped from Toledo in December 1967, and her body was found one month later in a traffic-heavy location several miles south of Ypsilanti. She had been raped and strangled with an electrical cord, in much the same manner as Dawn Basom. Her brassière was tied around her neck and her face had been bludgeoned with a hammer. The blows appeared consistent with the fractures sustained by Maralyn Skelton. Additionally, a three-inch nail had been driven into her skull, and the body had been stuffed inside a burlap sack.

Collins committed a series of brutal murders without the complications of empathy or guilt. Perhaps it is like he said: 'The perfect crime is when there is no guilt.' But the philosophy did not hold completely true. He believed that in the absence of guilt, a person could not get caught. Perhaps it is nothing more than a matter of semantics, but such distortions of reality are characteristic of all serial killers. For them, twisted meanings have legitimacy. For example, when asked if he was responsible for the death of Karen Sue Beineman, he insisted, 'No, I never met Karen Sue Beineman.' Several witnesses had placed the two of them together, and physical evidence proved that she was killed in his uncle's basement, yet he believed the play on words was enough to substantiate his innocence. Of course he had never met a person of that name. Assigning a name to her would only add personal qualities to an otherwise stereotypical presentation of the prop. Diners in a fine restaurant never assigned a name to the steak they were about to consume. The victims he killed were not people at all. In this manner, he could convince himself that he had never killed anyone. Such steadfast conviction serves as his intentional proof of deniability. It also amplifies his perception that an injustice has been committed against him. Like all the other narcissistic serial killers, he believes himself to be the victim.

Perhaps the scariest development in recent years is that Collins has been able to convince many people of his innocence. The evidence that convicted him was certainly strong, yet the same personality that had so effectively persuaded victims to let their guard down continues to convince many who visit him today that he is not the real Co-Ed Killer.

14. THE EVOLUTIONARY MODEL OF SERIAL MURDER

Imagine that you are an astronaut in the not-so-distant future. While you are exploring the galaxy, you come across a planet where all living creatures give off their own unique bands of ultraviolet light, which are perceptible to all other living creatures that are highly intuitive. These bands of UV light indicate to you that the majority of creatures on this planet are highly driven, highly intelligent, and highly independent of one another. They also possess an immense need for control, power and dominance. By comparing this to other planets you have explored, you discover that this planet is also the only one existing in a state of perpetual strife and hostility. The inhabitants seem either to have created their own branch of logical reasoning, or to have wholly abandoned any semblance of the concept. The race of beings that live on this planet are, for the most part, sadistic, and are not bound by any sense of social obligation to those who are not the same as they are. In fact, these dominant individuals live to prey on those who are weaker, not to mention that their victims are also more kind and socially attached to their fellow beings. How did this happen?

The answer, in part, was first postulated by Raymond Dart, a palaeontologist, in a paper entitled *The Predatory Transition From Ape To Man*, in which Dart suggests that man is the only member of the ape species who is a born killer. Fifteen million years ago, an ape discovered that he could kill those weaker than him by using a stone or a club. This made him a more efficient killer than those who preceded him. Carrying a club meant that the ape would need to walk upright on two feet. Hand-eye co-ordination would have to follow, and this meant further brain development. The dominance this creature, now known as the human, achieved was obtained through violence. Despite creating the most complex form of society ever known, man has been unable to rid himself of this instinct for killing. The unnatural feeling and stress of living in cramped quarters with other members of his species has led to increased levels and experiences of irritability and aggressiveness. The emergence of the serial killer is a further manifestation of this evolutionary process.

Throughout the history of the world, this process has been not only alluded to but also plainly revealed. From the crimes of Ivan the Terrible to those of Gilles de Rais, Adolf Hitler, and Theodore Robert Bundy, as well as countless others, we see that the increased levels of both security and comfort created by civilisation have also created a sense of boredom, longing, and a desire for sensation in those individuals who are more primal, more intelligent, and more aggressive than others.

Serial killers whose psychological characteristics and general make-up fit into the evolutionary model of serial murder commit their crimes out of the desire for self-assertion. The most noticeable traits of this type of serial killer are his need for recognition, his desire to create a legacy of fear, and, most significant of all, his overwhelming compulsion for committing crimes that not only defy all of conventional human logic, but also shock and intrigue. For a few weeks he becomes the talk of the entire world. His crimes appear on television and in magazines. Once apprehended and convicted, most serial killers have books written about them, with the most heinous of them being depicted by top-notch stars in made-for-TV movies. But while they may achieve status as a public celebrity, they are also frustrated by their position in the world, as they can only advance further by being caught.

The majority of the population, which does not commit serial homicide, moves through Maslow's hierarchy of values, which call for increased integration into society. Serial killers following the evolutionary path, in which they believe they are elevating themselves to a position above and beyond society and the normal bonds between individuals associated with it, are thinking and acting only for themselves. Science-fiction writer AE van Vogt has termed this type of individual 'the right man'. The 'right man', according to van Vogt, has an unhealthy and unnatural obsession with being right, as well as with making things right in his life. This usually involves compensating for some type of injustice he suffered, usually at a very young age and at the hands of someone who was or was supposed to be very close to him, according to normal societal relations. These individuals are devoid of the capacity for both self-criticism and self-reflection, are quick to blame others for their mistakes or shortcomings, and believe that the world owes them something, even though they insist they do not need it and claim to require no interaction or bond with the rest of the world. They also fly into rages without provocation and lack the capacity for proportional violence in relation to the situation they find themselves in. This type of serial killer is difficult to detect, as well as to profile accurately, because he does not recognise that his actions are nothing more than an exercise in self-indulgence. In reality, despite his efforts and actions, he has done nothing to elevate himself to a higher position on the food chain, but has in fact rather, by acting only on his primal urges, lowered himself a notch or two.

While struggling to assert himself, to demonstrate his independence and separation from society and societal norms, and thereby to evolve to a different form of human being, this type of serial killer is, in fact, innately tied to the society he is desperately attempting to sever ties with. This is because he is totally dependent upon the victim and the victim's reaction to both his fantasy and his actions, in order for his psychological foundations to remain stable. This type of serial killer exists within the wider pool of the dominant 5% of the population we hear so much about in the world of athletics, politics and business. Unlike the other members of this elite group who do not commit serial homicides, these individuals lack the qualities necessary to gain recognition from the rest of society. They have deluded themselves into believing that the only way for them to gain this recognition is to act on their fantasies and urges, thereby shunning the norms of society and evolving into creatures who need no one. They believe that they are not reliant on the approval of others – but this is only an illusion. Without the rest of society to recoil at the crimes of this type of serial offender, the person's entire life would be meaningless and he would exist forever in obscurity.

Murder itself has also evolved. Just as the emergence of the serial killer has had an impact on the normal functioning of everyday life in the 21st century, there has been a subtle, but nonetheless perceptible, change in the style of murder. While the industrial revolution brought great economic prosperity, it also brought a new form of self-consciousness, which had drastic effects on the psychology of those individuals who would eventually evolve into serial killers. The industrial revolution was, indeed, a form of rebellion, and with it a psychotic eruption followed, which changed the face of murder as it had hitherto been known.

Murder, from this point forward, lost its simple nature. No longer were victims isolated to predetermined categories involving spousal dissatisfaction or inheritance. Motives became more complex and tangled. This became the dominant factor of our time, in which murder began to have a dramatic impact on the conditions of human conduct, as well as society's inability to control it.

In such a complex mass society, it has become increasingly difficult for an individual to find some shred of human dignity and a sense of purpose as he attempts to create a meaning and structure for his life. Serial killers of the evolutionary model, because they lack the necessary prerequisites to succeed despite their innate capacity for dominance, are socially impotent and overwhelmed by the slightest hint of stress or frustration, which deeply throws their sense of self-importance off course.

These serial killers, neglected, sceptical, unable to escape the truth of their status and situation, abused, brain injured and afflicted with any of the other root causes of the disease of serial murder, seek purpose through their deviant and horrific acts. Powerless, these individuals can only hope to evolve to a level beyond humanity, where they will no longer be afflicted or confined by any of the bonds that they believe, rightly or wrongly, have thrust them into the state they currently inhabit. They have convinced themselves that there is no other answer, no other outlet for them to express their dominance, than to create a revolution by protesting against the war they imagine themselves to be fighting – a war against forces which are identifiable but also undefeatable.

What is most significant about this type of serial killer is that he suffers from a form of neurosis, which is an identifiable by-product of a raised level of expectation of the quality of the life experience. But these expectations are often left unfulfilled. The neurosis is further manifested in serial killers as what Charles Kingsley termed 'divine discontent'. This is a spur towards further enhancement of the standard of living, in which adverse environmental factors and events are eliminated. Such a lofty goal is achieved by the serial killer through repetitive stalking, kidnapping, torture, and the subsequent murder of victims. These behaviours symbolise a reaction against the factors and events that the serial killer believes have caused his poor quality of life. Because serial killers do not operate under the traditional sense of time, which would allow them the capacity to differentiate between distinct moments, they do not regard their victims as autonomous individuals but rather as disposable resources. This symbolic representation of victims can be found in all serial killers, regardless of what theory you ascribe to them. Because of this interpretation, the serial killer believes that by killing his victim, who is nothing but a physical representation of someone or something that has injured him, he is righting the wrongs that have been inflicted upon him. Therefore, he has corrected his life and created a better quality for it. It is this power, this ability to right injustices, which is at the heart of the evolutionary model of serial murder.

Serial killers of the evolutionary type are members of a class of people who could, if grouped together, define what might be termed a 'defensive society'. The environment of such a society would, no doubt, be hostile, and the individuals who would compose it, the serial killers, would be prepared to engage in destructive acts at the drop of a hat. Such groups of people would have few carefully controlled avenues for self-expression appropriate for life outside the community. In this way, they would have evolved according to the theory of defensive adaptation. Such displacement and lack of social interaction, as experienced by the serial killer of the evolutionary type, would provide only temporary comfort for the members of this society. They would be forced to seek satisfaction in other ways, and the main way for them to achieve this satisfaction would be to commit serial homicide.

To gain a better understanding of the type of serial killer we are dealing with when we are discussing the evolutionary model, it is important that we first recognise the fact that there is a continuous interaction between environmental stresses and the structure of an individual. By doing this, we open the door to a more accurate prediction of any subsequent responses the individual serial killer will exhibit towards any and all environmental transformations that may occur as a result of further social change.

The defensive society to which the serial killer belongs can be seen as an integral part of a specific type of revitalisation movement. This movement can be viewed as a concentrated effort to develop a more satisfying culture, stemming from the cumulative dissatisfactions experienced and exhibited by all serial killers of this type. Such a movement can be seen not only as evolutionary but also as emerging from a defensive process, which is initiated by feelings of hostility, frustration and stress. These factors are directly related to the differences between the actual and perceived social status of the serial killer, in correlation to his inherent dominance, and the flaws in his psychological, genetic and biological make-up, which prevent him from reaching his full potential as a productive social being.

Society's apparent worship of material goods and wealth has come to constitute, to a large extent, the very spirit of our times. This has led to feelings of effeminacy and unmanliness in the evolutionary serial killer because, despite his innate dominance within greater society, he is unable to achieve any of the goals society holds as precious. The war that rages inside the evolutionary serial killer demands an incredible effort to win, both in degree and duration. In reaction to this, the serial killer commits his crimes in what he believes to be a deterrent to the pain, discomfort, poverty and annoyance he has been forced to endure. It is through the looking glass of the theories of survival of the fittest and self-preservation that the evolutionary serial killer selects his victims. While symbolic of past injustices, his victims also represent membership in the group he views as weak and, therefore, in need of being eradicated.

In their minds, these killers have evolved to a higher stage of humanity because they not only recognise the need to eliminate the weaker portion of society, but also because they have the strength, courage and bravery to carry out such an act. Death becomes, in their minds, not only necessary but also commonplace. Thrusting conventional values and inhibitions aside in order to evolve, this type of serial killer moves forwards with a new-found energy and is freed, to a certain extent, by his perceived elevation to a higher plane of power that he can exercise over those he believes to be inferior.

For this type of serial killer, the society he has disassociated himself from is composed of nothing but weak, sneaky slaves to a system that prevents growth and the reaching of one's true potential. But these weaker individuals pose the greatest threat to this type of serial offender, for it is this group, and not other evolutionary serial killers, that becomes the killer's undoing. The evolutionary serial killer cannot resolve the paradox that these individuals place their own existence in jeopardy. Society serves as a mirror for the evolutionary killer, and he believes he has risen above its reflection. Yet this mirror is a constant reminder of what he could become, as well as where he came from. Therefore, it must be shattered and eliminated.

Along with what has already been stated above, there are at least nine diagnosable symptoms that evolutionary serial killers exhibit. These symptoms are present to an elevated extent, with a pronounced level of intensity, in this group. They may not be as significant in other types of serial offenders, who display the same category of symptoms to a lesser extent. These are as follows:

1. Engagement in repeated patterns of ritualistic behaviour
2. Obsessive and compulsive behaviours
3. Extreme memory disorders
4. A documented criminal history of assault and other lesser offences
5. Hypersexuality
6. Neurological impairments
7. Genetic disorders
8. Biochemical deficiencies
9. Extreme feelings of inadequacy

Ritualistic behaviour can be seen across the entire spectrum of serial murderers, regardless of which model they follow. In the evolutionary type of serial killer, however, this sort of behaviour is characterised by the fact that it forms the basis of the serial killer's personality, and is evident to others long before the commission of the first murder. Rituals are repeatable, observable patterns of behaviour exhibited by the serial killer, which bind him to his crimes. Any deviation from the ritual, either before, during, or after the commission of a murder, is not representative of the evolutionary type of serial killer, but is indicative of outside events or factors beyond the serial killer's control. Such factors serve only as causative elements in any alteration of the ritual.

The engagement in compulsive behaviour, in and of itself, is not indicative of any form of deviance. In the evolutionary type of serial killer, however, we see patterns of compulsion and obsession, which manifest themselves in more than one way. One way in which this type of offender exhibits compulsive behaviour is in his record-keeping. This type of killer not only maintains meticulous records regarding his crimes, following them closely in the media and returning to the crime scene, but also maintains similar records about every other aspect of their lives, of which most 'normal' people do not keep records. This compulsive activity usually contributes to the prosecution's case against such a killer. It also contributes to an answer to the curious question of why serial killers of this type become model prisoners once incarcerated.

Obsessive attention to detail and compulsion, relating to the evolutionary serial killer's daily, mundane activities, represent a behavioural set of symptoms which are indicators of a person suffering from feelings of intense anger and instability regarding their mental state of health. Such manifestations of personal emotional rigidity appear early in development, and if caught and treated can help to prevent the emergence of this type of serial offender.

Evolutionary serial killers are predisposed to developing into pathological liars. While most serial killers are untrustworthy and often lie when confronted with their crimes, the evolutionary type of serial predator lies about every aspect of his life. So deeply do these falsehoods penetrate into every aspect of his life that he will even lie about details which are trivial and inconsequential. For the serial offender, truth does not conform to the same definition that it holds for the majority of the population. Since this type of murderer has evolved to shun all of what normal society has to offer, truth becomes whatever he wants or needs it to be in order for him to survive.

It is discovered, once evolutionary serial killers are apprehended, that they characteristically possess a long criminal record for serious acts of physical assault. The assaults are documented from much earlier in their lives than is typically seen in other serial killers with similar records. From a very early age, the evolutionary serial killer recognises that he is different from those around him, and these differences cause him to act in physically aggressive ways.

Hypersexuality is another symptom that is generally exhibited by most serial killers. In the evolutionary type of serial murderer, this hypersexuality takes on a life of its own. After several years of the killer fantasising about and then committing murder, this abnormality manifests itself to such an overwhelming extent that it appears as if a split has developed in the killer's mental state. While far short of the so-called 'multiple personality syndrome' claimed by some serial killers as a defence for their actions, this split is quite real and has been documented in the cases of such serial killers as Ted Bundy. His hypersexuality is best illustrated by the way in which he returned to the burial sites of his victims, dug up the bodies and had sex with the corpses. This exploration of necrophilia became an addiction, in which he needed to continue murdering in order to replenish his supply of bodies. In addition to this, Bundy spent a relatively long period of time with his victims before killing them, often keeping them alive for several days to gratify his fantasies. While this was happening, he maintained several 'normal' relationships with girlfriends, in which he engaged in sexual activity of a more 'regular' nature. The hypersexual side of the evolutionary serial offender grabs control of the rest of the psychological mechanisms of the individual to the point where nothing else exists but the desire for sex. It is this split that leads to the evolutionary serial killer's downward spiral, which ultimately leads to his capture.

Symptoms of severe neurological impairment manifest themselves in the form of hard signs in the evolutionary serial killer, as opposed to the soft signs of such impairment discovered in serial killers of other types. These hard signs include confusing right and left, reversing letters or numbers, and learning disabilities of the sort which are associated with behavioural problems.

Some researchers, including Dr Joel Norris, have made the assertion that individuals who display between three and five physical anomalies also have a genetic disorder of the primal brain. The correlation between the two stems from the physiological link between the development of the fetal brain and the rate of time it takes for the skin to develop. Since the development of the fetal brain occurs at the same time as that of the skin, any anomalies in the skin or cartilage are indicators that the brain has not developed as it should either. This condition is most profound in the evolutionary type of serial killer, who tends to exhibit more than five such anomalies. These serial killers include Ted Bundy, Randy Kraft and Kenneth McDuff. Such anomalies include, but are not limited to, wiry hair that will not comb down, bulbous fingertips, a head circumference outside the normal range, deformities in the ears, webbed skin and abnormalities in the teeth.

The biochemical symptoms that afflict the evolutionary serial killer extend beyond those of other serial offenders, with respect to the way in which their bodies and immune systems cast off toxins that are either ingested voluntarily, or enter the body through other means. The evolutionary type of serial killer, due to his genetic abnormalities, is also saddled with an immune system that cannot rid his body of toxic compounds or substances. These biochemical symptoms have nothing to do with those exhibited by serial killers who fall under the umbrella of the medical model discussed in an earlier chapter.

Finally, the evolutionary serial killer, like most other serial offenders, suffers from severe feelings of inadequacy. In this type of serial murderer, it is this very feeling that causes him to evolve into a killer, while in other serial killers these feelings are more directly associated with the crimes themselves.

While it would be easy to misinterpret the patterns and symptoms that the evolutionary serial killer exhibits as absolute predictors for future criminal behaviour, this is not the intention of the model. The evolutionary model of serial murder is one more tool in the quest to understand the behaviour and actions of such offenders, and should be taken only to provide a possible direction and structure for future multi-disciplinary research.

15. RANDY KRAFT

The crimes and murders committed by Randy Kraft began on New Year's Eve, 1975. By 1983, Kraft had committed over one hundred murders, a staggering number of homicides that makes him the poster child for American serial murder. He was eventually convicted of sixteen murders and sentenced to death. Carrying out his sentence at San Quentin State Penitentiary, Kraft plays bridge and interacts with other serial killers such as Douglas Clark, Lawrence Bittaker and, before his death in 2002, William Bonin.

Randy Kraft was born on 19 March 1945, at the beginning of what has become known as the 'Baby Boom'. He suffered from several injuries as a child, many of which were caused by a series of falls. Soon after his first birthday, Kraft fell off the couch in his family's living room, and at the age of two, he fell down a set of concrete steps, a tumble off the family porch that left him unconscious. In addition to the severe head injuries Kraft suffered in his early youth, he was also born with several genetic abnormalities, including an enlarged head circumference and lowered ear lobes. These conditions are indicators that the brain did not develop as it should have. In normal development, the fetal brain grows at the same rate as the foetus's skin. In Kraft's case, this did not appear to have happened.

An exceptionally gifted individual, Kraft was saddled with a family that had, at best, minimal means of support. Randy's father, Harold Kraft, worked on an assembly line and struggled to support his wife and children. The financial strain became so great on the Kraft family that Randy's mother, Opal, had to take a position as a sewing-machine operator, which left little time for nurturing bonds to form between Randy and either of his parents.

In 1963, Kraft graduated from Westminster High School. His academic performance for those four years saw him ranked tenth out of nearly four hundred students and earned him a scholarship to the exclusive Claremont Men's College. Randy Kraft would later remark that, after an initial period of apprehension, he realised he was a homosexual during his years at Westminster High. But it was not until 1975 that his parents became aware of their son's sexual orientation. Harold Kraft refused to accept the fact that his son was gay, while Opal Kraft, a devout member of the Presbyterian faith, refused to acknowledge that her son was different from other young men his age.

Already frustrated by the fact that his family's social and economic status prevented him from achieving his rightful place in society as one of the dominant 5% of the population, Kraft had further reason to sever his ties with normal society and its inhabitants due to the way in which his family and others looked upon homosexuals in the 1970s. Forced to hide his sexual urges and desires from those around him, Kraft had no other choice but to retreat into a world of fantasy where it was safe to express himself and the feelings he had about the other young men he spent his time with at Claremont. In 1964, Kraft further alienated himself from his family and friends by declaring that he was an atheist. The announcement must have come as a slap in the face to his mother, who had raised him in a fanatically religious manner.

While in college, Kraft took a series of low-paying jobs tending bar in some of the prevalently gay bars throughout the area. He had several homosexual affairs with strange men, but began to resent his homosexuality. It was not long before he began to take this insecurity out on others, particularly the men he had become intimately involved with. It was during this period of his life that Kraft began to disappear for long periods of time, leaving no indication of where he had gone. When asked where he had been, Kraft would refuse to answer. It was at this time that he completely severed himself from the need for social interaction, and began to evolve into one of the most vicious serial killers of our time. This transformation took place as a result of several factors from his early childhood and teenage years. Feelings of inadequacy, coupled with the rejection of others, had created a new identity – that of a monster.

The transformation began in response to psychological turmoil, but also presented some significant physical symptoms. Physiological signs of his illness appeared in the early to mid-1960s, when Kraft began to suffer from severe, chronic headaches and stomach-aches. Although he was prescribed hundreds of different forms of medication for his symptoms, nothing seemed to work. This, I believe, is a clear illustration that he was undergoing some sort of psychosomatic change, in which the part of him that was still clinging to humanity was fighting against his latent sexual urges. But ultimately, Randy Kraft's humanity lost the battle, and he subsequently evolved into America's most prolific serial killer.

In 1966, Kraft solicited an undercover police officer for sex on a Huntington Beach pier and received a warning. The warning, however, did not serve its purpose, and Kraft continued to solicit and have sex with strange men throughout the Huntington Beach area. Some of these incidents were violent, with Kraft usually playing the aggressor. His hypersexuality and overwhelming obsession with sex detracted from his college studies, and he received a D in an econometrics class, which prevented him from graduating with the rest of his class in the spring of 1967. He did not receive his diploma from Claremont Men's College until February 1968, when he received a degree in economics.

Later that year, Kraft entered the United States Air Force and received a secret security clearance to work at the Air Force Flight Test Center at Edwards Air Force Base, Southern California, as a protective-coating specialist. Kraft quickly rose to the rank of airman first class and became a supervising manager at the base. But once again, he felt snubbed by his relatively low status on the food chain and complained vehemently about what he perceived to be injustices committed against him by the United States Government. Kraft wrote several letters during this time, in which he complained about being humiliated by being forced to work with others at the base who were clearly beneath him. He also mentioned the difficulties he had in getting along with his peers and fellow workers. In 1969, Kraft decided to put an end to his military service and take the next step in the evolution of a serial killer. He informed his superior officers at the base that he was homosexual. On 26 July 1969, a little over a year after he had enlisted, Randy Kraft was discharged from the Air Force for what were listed as medical reasons.

Things quickly deteriorated for Kraft after his discharge from the military. In March 1970 he approached thirteen-year-old Joey Fancher, a runaway, and asked him if he needed a place to stay. Once inside Kraft's apartment, the young boy was given eight pills and some alcohol, and immediately became disoriented. Kraft physically assaulted and sodomised him, then, after threatening the boy with death, left for work. Taking advantage of his absence, the boy managed to escape from the apartment. He was taken to a hospital and told police about the attack. Investigators followed the boy back to Kraft's apartment and found jars full of Benzedrine, Seconal and marijuana. The pills, some of which were sedatives and anti-depressants, were believed to be what had knocked Joey Fancher out before Kraft attacked him. They also uncovered a stack of 76 snapshots of Kraft and other men in various poses of sexual activity.

Despite the eyewitness account and the evidence located in Kraft's apartment, police did not take Joey Fancher or his tale very seriously. They believed that he had accompanied Kraft to the apartment, had taken the pills voluntarily, and had been looking for trouble. Since he was a runaway, they felt inclined to disbelieve him. They never pursued any charges against Kraft, but it is evident from this, and other similar incidents involving him, that fantasising about sex and violence no longer satisfied him. Kraft began acting out his fantasies.

By late 1974, police had several unsolved homicide cases on their hands, all with similar modus operandi and the same ritual signature. No suspects had been arrested in these cases, which included the deaths of Vincent Cruz Mestas, Malcolm Eugene Little, Roger E. Dickerson, Thomas Paxton Lee, Gary Wayne Cordova and James Dale Reeves. All the victims were either known or suspected homosexuals, all were nude and mutilated, and had been sexually assaulted; all had had items stuck into their anuses, and all had died from a combination of asphyxiation, alcohol, and drug ingestion.

A talented computer programmer at a time when computers were not as readily available as they are today, Kraft was familiar with all aspects of computer engineering and maintenance. The choice to work in a field that was still in its infancy, and yet excelling far above the standards of many other occupations, was another sign of Kraft's evolution to a higher stage of humanity. But despite his talents, motivation, and abilities with computers, Kraft lost several jobs in the field because of lay-offs or minor infractions of company policy. In the summer of 1980, Kraft was let go from his job at Lear Siegler, partly because of the lack of work, but also in part because during one weekend trip to Portland in July 1980 on company business, Kraft had run up almost a thousand miles on a rented Lincoln Town Car from Hertz. The distance between the airport where he was staying and the company where he was working was only 25 miles. Again, Kraft had no explanation for this obvious and large discrepancy. His refusal to answer Lear Siegler's request for information was an assertion of his determination to separate himself from the rest of society. This reflected his opinion that he was better than everyone else, and therefore did not feel the need to answer to anyone.

By 1983, at the age of 37, Randy Kraft continued to suffer from the symptoms of his mysterious illness. They had grown worse, and included bumping into things, fainting, trouble with writing, driving and vision, as well as weakness in his knees, chest pains, headaches, numbness in his extremities, and a pounding, pulse-like sensation throughout his entire body. A treadmill test revealed that he had a rapid, irregular and skipped heartbeat, which could be attributed to the fact that Kraft smoked two packs of cigarettes a day. The other symptoms could not be explained medically.

For years, Kraft had been carrying on a relationship with a man named Jeff Graves, who was several years younger. Though the existence of such a relationship may be falsely accredited to Kraft's ostensible desire to maintain social relationships, a further, and more detailed, examination of this relationship demonstrates that it is consistent with the evolutionary model of serial murder proposed in an earlier chapter. Kraft secretly despised Graves for several reasons, which he attempted to hide from Graves and only revealed after his apprehension. Kraft believed that Graves, like most of society, was using him. He believed that Graves was taking from him without giving anything in return. Kraft could not abide this because his partner clearly inhabited a place beneath him. He blamed Graves for his illness, which he claimed had been brought about by the stress resulting from an imbalance of status – he considered this to be a significant level of stress, considering that he was evolving and that Graves was holding him back from becoming the man he was intended to become. Finally, the Kraft–Graves relationship became one in which Kraft kept Graves as subservient as possible. This again supports the theory that Kraft was severed from society, despite his engagement in a relationship.

Around one o'clock in the morning on 14 May 1983, California Highway Patrol officers pulled over a 1979 Toyota Celica in the town of Mission Viejo, along Interstate 5. The car was pulled over for erratic driving, as officers had witnessed it weave on and off the shoulder of the road. Initially officers turned on their lights, but not their sirens. The driver refused to stop. Instead, he reached into the back seat and retrieved a jacket, which he threw over the passenger side of the vehicle. The police turned on the sirens and ordered the driver to pull over, using the public address system. The Toyota then pulled over to the side of the road and Randy Kraft emerged, heading towards the police cruiser. After a field sobriety test revealed that Kraft was driving under the influence of alcohol, police handcuffed him and placed him under arrest. They then approached Kraft's vehicle and noticed that there was a young man sitting in the passenger seat. Believing him to be asleep, officers attempted to wake the man using various means, but when these efforts were unsuccessful one of them entered the car through the driver's side and noticed several pill vials and empty bottles of beer. Officer Michael Howard then attempted to wake the passenger by touching him, only to realise that he was dead. He located a five inch Buck knife in the front seat and placed it immediately into evidence.

Terry Lee Gambrel, a 25-year-old Marine, had his wrists bound with his shoelaces and his penis and testicles exposed when police discovered his body in Randy Kraft's car. Marks on Gambrel's neck were consistent with those of strangulation, and had been made with his own belt. When paramedics arrived, they asked Kraft what might have given Gambrel the heart attack he had apparently suffered. Kraft answered that he had given the young man some Ativan.

Once in custody, Kraft refused to give a statement without having a lawyer present. A search warrant was issued for Kraft's Toyota. Inside, investigators found nine different prescription medications, an envelope full of 47 photos of dead men, and a blood-soaked passenger seat. Even though this was where Gambrel had been sitting, his body showed no evidence of open wounds. Kraft had obviously used the vehicle to cart other trophies from place to place. Inside the trunk of the car, police located a binder with a tablet containing 61 printed notations, which appeared to be in code. The list was deciphered to include what police believed in total to be the names of 65 victims who had fallen prey to the diseased mind and evolutionary desire of Randy Kraft.

The search continued inside Kraft's home, where police discovered even more terrifying evidence. This included items of property belonging to several different men who were known to be missing, bloodstained walls, and enough clothing, rugs and furniture to fill an entire moving van.

The now famous list consisted of half a single sheet, torn from a yellow legal pad. There were 30 names or phrases on the left side of the page, and 31 on the far right. Kraft explained it as a list of nicknames he had given to his associates within the gay community. Police discovered that it was actually a score-card. Each entry represented a victim, for whom the code described a certain aspect of personal identification that Kraft wished to preserve. The code provided a strong piece of evidence, as it could be linked to missing persons in a variety of states in which Kraft had travelled. But it was also quite complex. Six years after Kraft was arrested, only two-thirds of it had been deciphered. Of the 61 entries, 41 were tied to men who had been killed between 1971 and 1983. There are still twenty entries on the list which continue to perplex investigators. The final count, police decided, was 67 deaths, over a period of 12½ years.

The maintenance of the list, as well as that of other documents, and the meticulous way in which Kraft tended to both his appearance and his home, are indicative of the type of obsessive-compulsive behaviour we see in serial killers of the evolutionary type. These characteristics point to a well-organised mind that strives to maintain order and a sense of stability in its world, a world that is often chaotic and painful as the evolutionary process moves towards fruition.

Randy Kraft maintains his innocence to this day. On 27 September 1983, after five postponements and an attempt by Kraft's defence to close the trial to the public, the preliminary hearing regarding the case began. Kraft's lawyer, Fred McBride, would eventually quit the defence team after Kraft publicly berated his style. Doug Otto also left, after Kraft insisted on acting as co-counsel. By April 1986, Randy Kraft had been in prison for three years without having a trial. Over the next five years, his defence team was granted twelve additional delays. By 1985, Kraft was charged with sixteen murders in California, two in Michigan, and six in Oregon. In the summer of 1988, jury selection finally began with the mailing of a staggering fifteen thousand summonses.

At last, on 26 September 1988, Randy Kraft was granted his day in court. The trial had a ten million dollar price tag, seven hundred witnesses, and two hundred and fifty exhibits. Despite the legal battles waged on his behalf, on 12 May 1989, only eleven days after the trial ended, Randy Kraft was found guilty of sixteen counts of first-degree murder. One day later, he was sentenced to die.

There are many interesting points about Randy Kraft and his evolution into the most accomplished serial killer in American history. He emerged from a normal family, which by all accounts was considered to be loving and protective. But Randy Kraft was born into the portion of the population known as the dominant 5%, and his humble upbringing brought him little more than frustration. Douglas Clark, a contemporary who shares California's death row, has become one of his closest friends. When asked to describe him, Clark observed, 'Kraft is a slightly more gay-acting version of Ted Bundy.' But throughout his life, Kraft's homosexuality also frustrated him, and he was forced to rely on fantasies which involved the intermingling of sex and violence to satisfy his sexual desires. Kraft, in the evolutionary mode, displayed an irresponsible and self-centred attitude, which was highlighted by his total indifference to the welfare of other members of society. He was methodical to the point of obsession, and his detailed accounts of his crimes in the form of the list were what led, in part, to his criminal convictions.

As a result of the head injuries that Kraft suffered during the first two years of his life, it was inevitable that he would develop obsessive-compulsive behaviours. But to the casual observer, these behaviours would not make him appear outwardly abnormal. While the brain damage he suffered from the fall off the porch and down the concrete steps in his childhood left him susceptible to the type of uncontrolled and unfettered emotional outbursts he exhibited during his sexual assaults and murders, he was still capable of maintaining a façade of normality. This allowed him to live an otherwise productive and somewhat successful life.

The mutilation of his victims points to the fact that he did not view them as people, and in fact, for Kraft, they were not people. Since he had evolved and they were beneath him, they did not deserve any recognition of their human condition. The mutilation also points to the fact that he was ashamed of his homosexuality and had to remove his victims' genitals to make them female, which made him feel better about having sex with them. By destroying his victims, Kraft was destroying all the elements in himself that he considered to be weak. Such perceived weaknesses prevented him from achieving all the things he felt he was rightly entitled to receive. By committing his murders, and by symbolically destroying those elements which made him human and weak, he could fully evolve above the normal human race. This evolutionary experience explains, in part, why Kraft enjoys prison so much. In such a place, he is surrounded by his equals, others like him, who evolved, and no longer fear society. Rising above society's limits, he can finally deal with the wrongs that have been committed against him, whether they are real or imaginary.

16. KENNETH ALLEN MCDUFF

Kenneth Allen McDuff was born in Paris, Texas to John Allen and Addie McDuff. John McDuff was a farmer and his wife stayed at home and controlled every aspect of her family's life, from the money to the discipline. She utilised the domineering personality with which she had been endowed to its fullest and most detrimental capacity. One of the biggest problems that Kenneth McDuff had when he was a boy, which contributed to his lifelong pattern of believing that there were no rules that applied to him, was that his mother refused to believe that her son could ever do anything wrong or against the law, even when proof in the form of physical evidence was provided to her. Her laidback and perhaps overly protective attitude, which caused her to live in denial of her son's wrongdoing, served as a catalyst for a crime and murder spree that began when Kenneth was very young.

Constantly in trouble with the law and with neighbours while he was still in grade school, McDuff learned quickly that no matter what he said to his mother, or how outlandish his excuses were, she would always believe him, stand by him, and defend him. McDuff, according to official reports, had difficulty getting along with his peers, teachers, and just about everyone else. Throughout his youth and later into adulthood, the future serial killer would lie, steal, and destroy the property of others with what seemed to be reckless and remorseless abandon. Suffering from academic problems and failures which were probably the result of an undiagnosed and untreated learning disability, McDuff tested just above the mentally retarded range on several achievement tests in the lower grades. Informed that her son might not be as perfect as she had come to believe, Addie McDuff vehemently denied that her son was disabled and refused to allow him to be evaluated further. This was the first step in McDuff's evolution into a serial killer.

Large for his age, McDuff learned that because of his size he could intimidate others and force them to do whatever he wanted them to. These early seeds of the need for dominance and control, coupled with a permissive mother, allowed McDuff to create fantasies in which he was king of the world and could have whatever and whoever he wanted, because he was strong and not under the control of any laws or rules. From the sixth grade to the ninth, Kenneth McDuff was known as a colossal discipline problem who missed a great deal of school because he was often suspended for fighting and other infractions of school rules. McDuff, fed up with school and believing that he could be whatever he wanted, even without an education, dropped out after the ninth grade. His IQ at the time was measured at 92, but he was a huge failure academically. This did not phase McDuff, and nor did the fact that he had difficulty reading, until the day he was executed by the state of Texas.

If there was anyone who Kenneth McDuff ever truly bonded with in his life, it was his brother Lonnie. Because Kenneth did not have any friends, his brother was the only one he ever respected. The brothers got along well because they shared the same false sense of invulnerability engendered by their mother's attitude towards them. Nothing they ever did was wrong, simply because of the fact that they were the ones who did it. The only truth was that which came out of their own mouths, and the only things that were correct and proper were the things that they believed to be so. Both brothers were excessively and unhealthily egocentric. While they each had their own belongings that could never be touched or borrowed by anyone else, they felt and acted as though they could take the possessions of those around them without so much as a second thought. Others only existed to listen to, obey and serve them. One of Kenneth McDuff's favourite pastimes was to harass smaller boys until they wet themselves.

Upon dropping out of school, Kenneth McDuff took a job with his father pouring concrete. By the age of fifteen McDuff was an alcoholic, and he began committing a string of robberies in 1964. On 17 April that year, he was taken into custody for these crimes, and by January the following year he had been convicted of car theft, as well as thirteen other counts of theft and burglary across three separate counties. Despite the fact that he received thirteen four-year prison sentences, the judge declared that they would run concurrently, so he would only technically have to serve a maximum of four years. Taken to jail in March 1965, he was paroled for the first time nine months later, in December 1965.

Roy Dale Green had the unfortunate luck to meet and befriend McDuff in July 1966. It was only five days after Charles Whitman had murdered fourteen people from the tower at the University of Texas in Austin, and McDuff and his new friend headed to Fort Worth. After drinking several six-packs of beer, McDuff spotted a 1955 Ford near the baseball field of Everman High School. He withdrew a Colt revolver from his vehicle, ordered Green to get the stick he kept in the back seat, and instructed him to follow. Approaching the Ford, McDuff spotted two teenage boys and a girl. He robbed them of their wallets at gunpoint, then placed the three terrified youths into the trunk of their own car. McDuff then ordered Green to follow them in McDuff's Ford. Green did what he was told, never once realising that he could have saved the three teenagers by driving to the nearest police station.

McDuff carefully selected a semi-secluded farm-to-market road numbered FM 1017 for the spot where he would commit his first murders. He first removed the young girl he had taken hostage and placed her inside the trunk of his car. Proceeding with methodical precision, he then executed the two teenage boys in the trunk of the Ford, firing a total of five shots. In an attempt to shove the dead bodies of the two boys back into the trunk, McDuff grew infuriated because one of the boy's legs got caught, preventing the trunk from closing all the way. Rather than run from the scene in a panic, he regained his composure and carefully backed the Ford up against a fence, so that the opened trunk and its grisly cargo could not be easily seen from the side of the road. Both Green and McDuff wiped the car clean of prints and McDuff made sure he had flattened out all of the tyre tracks that had been made by the Ford and the Dodge.

Now driving his own car with Green seated on the passenger side, McDuff pulled the vehicle onto a more secluded gravel road, removed his teenage captive from the trunk, and placed her in the back seat. Roy Green watched as Kenneth McDuff viciously raped the young girl, then raped her himself at McDuff's command. After raping her a second time, McDuff sexually assaulted her with the jagged end of a broken broomstick he had found. The girl was told to put her clothes back on, and after they had driven to another road she was ordered to get out of the vehicle, and was thrown to the ground. McDuff then crushed the bones in her neck with the broomstick he had used earlier. She died after a violent struggle, and her lifeless body was then tossed over a barbed-wire fence, dragged into a clump of trees, and covered in brush. The act of murder was the second step in McDuff's rapid evolution into a serial killer.

After disposing of the young girl's body, McDuff and Green got rid of the wallets and broomstick. The next morning, McDuff buried the gun he had used in a hole dug near Roy Green's garage. Once they had washed the car, both inside and out, Green was dropped off at his home by McDuff, who never had the slightest idea that Green had been so terrified by the murders that as soon as he got the chance he would run to the police, which is exactly what he did. Green's confession led to an all-out manhunt for McDuff and the body of his female victim. Green led police to the body of the young girl, while other officers apprehended Kenneth McDuff, after a car chase that resulted in several rounds being fired into his vehicle.

Kenneth McDuff's parole was revoked on 9 August 1966, and he found himself back in jail for the murders of the three teenagers. Despite the fact that McDuff's mother, Addie, had concocted a fraudulent alibi, claiming that at the time of the murders he had been with a young woman whose name she could not reveal because the young woman went to their church, McDuff was put on trial for the murders. His defence was that Roy Green had committed the crimes and his role had been only secondary in the attacks. McDuff claimed that at the time of the murder he had been asleep in the parking lot of a burned-out shopping centre, and that his only involvement had been in assisting Green to dispose of the bodies. Despite the fact that the revolver and the broomstick were never produced by the prosecution, Kenneth McDuff was found guilty of the murders and sentenced to death for the first time on 15 November 1966. He was set to be executed in December 1968, but following the ruling in the case of Furman vs Georgia, his life was spared and his sentence commuted to life in prison. Unbelievably, this sentence carried with it the possibility of parole.

While in prison, McDuff continued to evolve into the serial killer whose infamy would spread far and wide, through communication with other murderers and career criminals. He received his GED and earned 45 hours of college credit. Despite these achievements, McDuff used the prison to smuggle in drugs and soon became a steady dealer of illegal narcotics while inside. Then everything began to collapse for the state of Texas, and a series of errors and foul play would lead to McDuff being paroled for a second time. In the case of the murder of the young girl, McDuff's attorney filed a Writ for a Quick and Speedy Trial. It was denied because it was incorrectly filed by the courthouse as a Writ of Habeas-Corpus. Since his constitutional rights had been violated, both the murder and rape charges filed against him in the case were formally dismissed in March 1978.

Exactly three years later, Kenneth McDuff attempted to bribe the parole commissioner by guaranteeing that the commissioner would find ten thousand dollars in the glove compartment of his car if parole were granted. This first attempt at bribing a parole-board official was unsuccessful. It was not until January 1988 that McDuff succeeded in winning parole, but it was rescinded by the board after they received several hundred angry letters from people in the community who were outraged over the possibility. This did not seem to phase McDuff, whose attorney and mother incorporated a business called 'Justice for McDuff, Inc.' As part of the plan for his parole, they pursued both a book and movie deal. The year 1989 also marked the fifteenth time that Kenneth McDuff had sat in front of the Texas Parole Board. On 1 September 1989, he received the two votes he needed to be paroled, after almost twenty-three years behind bars. He walked out of prison a free man on 11 October 1989, and promptly took the position of vice-president at the company founded by his attorney and his mother.

It was not long before Kenneth McDuff found himself behind bars again. In September 1990, his parole was revoked because he had threatened a high-school student with a knife. Unfortunately for McDuff's future victims, an administrative decision to reinstate McDuff's parole took place only three months later. This time, it happened because his accusers in the incident never showed up at the parole revocation hearing to confirm their accounts of what had happened on the night in question.

Free, once again, to terrorise the inhabitants of the state of Texas, McDuff began to do so immediately. He dated several prostitutes, with whom he had rough sex, often inflicting physical and sexual abuse on them. He also robbed grocery stores and stole from other businesses whenever the urge took him. As had been the case during most of his previous criminal career, McDuff behaved erratically without rhyme or reason, as he continued to evolve into a serial killer.

He acted without emotion and did not enjoy the sexual intercourse he had with the prostitutes he dated. Sex was another way for him to inflict pain upon other human beings, and that is why he engaged in it. This is significant to the evolutionary model, because it demonstrates how disconnected and distanced McDuff had become from other people. He no longer interacted with anyone as though they were human beings, and even began to shun his mother. McDuff became totally egocentric, evolving to the stage of existence in which he was the only one that mattered. Others were only there to serve him, and existed solely in terms of what he could get or take from them. While most serial killers are loners and antisocial, they do, to some degree, characteristically maintain a few superficial relationships with people in order to hide their crimes from the rest of society. They may not recognise that their victims are people, but they at least, unlike McDuff, recognise that there are such things as other people in the world.

Further evidence of McDuff's evolution can be seen in the types of environments in which he chose to prowl. Always stalking those who existed on the fringe, and intermingling in several different subcultures, McDuff, unlike other serial killers who choose these fields of play because they can find easy prey inside them, did so because it made him feel even more superior. It put him closer to being God, at least in his mind. Being better than those around him did not take much of an effort, considering that he surrounded himself with what most of society would consider marginal or forgotten people, those who were perhaps no longer worthy of human respect and recognition. Once this stage of the evolutionary process was complete, having placed himself in the position of God and believing in that reality, he no longer gained satisfaction from his twisted fantasies of power and control. McDuff had no other choice but to begin committing more murders, in order to solidify in his mind his belief that he was God and could do whatever he wanted.

Kenneth McDuff started college in January 1991 at Texas State Technical Institute in Waco. He occupied a single room on campus and took courses which allowed him to pursue other activities. He distanced himself from other people. The courses were competency-based, requiring that McDuff demonstrate certain skills. Regular attendance was therefore not required, as it would have been with more academically oriented classes. He graduated from the school two years later with a 3.364 GPA and had made the Dean's Honor Roll on at least one occasion.

Brenda Thompson met up with McDuff, one of her regular customers on 10 October 1991. Only this time, prostitution was not the only order of business. It would be their last meeting, as he murdered her that night. Police could have apprehended McDuff before Thompson's murder, since he ran a roadblock and was chased by police, only to outrun them. Thompson had been seen inside McDuff's truck, bound and kicking violently against the glass of the passenger side window and front windshield. An incident report was never filed, despite the fact that McDuff had aimed his truck at several police officers and attempted to run them over as he evaded the roadblock. Police claimed that no report was filed and that there was no search for the offender because officers had not feared for their lives as a result of the incident.

Regenia DeAnn Moore had an encounter with McDuff about a week after he murdered Brenda Thompson. She, too, was murdered by the serial killer. Moore's death was followed by that of Colleen Reed on 29 December 1991. This time, McDuff raped the young girl with a man named Alva Hank Worley, in a similar situation to that which had occurred between McDuff and Roy Dale Green, except that Worley never reported the crime to the police. McDuff received a two year suspended sentence for public intoxication charges on 24 February 1992, placing him on both parole and probation simultaneously. At around the same time, he murdered Valencia Kay Joshua.

Kenneth McDuff had a rough day on 1 March 1992, or so he claimed. First, his car had broken down and required eight hundred dollars in repairs, which left him penniless. His cigarettes had been stolen and he had not been hired for a job that he had thought he was certain to get. He had been smoking crack the night before and had had a fight with his mother. Angry and in need of a fix, McDuff left his mother's home and abducted Melissa Northrup from a Quick Pak store. Spotted by several passers-by, McDuff, with Northrup already in the vehicle, stole her car and headed out of Central Texas. He drove over a hundred miles to Combine, Texas, where he bound Northrup, raped her repeatedly, then murdered her and threw her lifeless body into a flooded gravel pit.

The ease and success with which Kenneth McDuff committed his crimes only served to reinforce in his mind the idea that he could do no wrong. It also reinforced and served as a catalyst for McDuff's continued evolution as a serial killer, constantly serving as a reminder that he did not need anyone, and that others were there solely for the purpose of allowing him to meet his own needs. However, he was lulled so far into a false sense of security by the ease of this evolutionary rise to the status of serial killer that he did not realise that by stealing Northrup's car and leaving his own vehicle at the Quik Pak, he was leaving behind some valuable evidence for the police. It was this evidence that eventually led to his arrest and incarceration.

A federal warrant was drawn up on 6 March 1992, stemming from drugs charges that had been filed against him for activities he had engaged in while attending college in Waco. Gun charges were also filed against him, and he became a fugitive wanted by the ATF. Three days later, an arrest warrant was drawn up for McDuff by the state of Texas for parole violations. Inside the trunk of McDuff's vehicle, investigators located several pieces of valuable evidence, among them hair samples and what appeared to be blood. McDuff knew that he was a wanted man and attempted to hide out for as long as he could, but in the end his efforts at avoiding capture were unsatisfactory because he had deluded himself into believing that he was invincible and would never actually be arrested. This is a common flaw within the thought patterns of those killers who fit into the evolutionary model of serial murder. Unlike other serial killers, who similarly may not believe on a conscious level that they will be caught, subconsciously they wish to be apprehended. This causes them to do things in their later – and often final – crimes that practically lead the police to their front door.

McDuff spent most of the early part of March, following Northrup's murder, at several shelters in Missouri. He eventually landed a job as a garbageman and moved into an apartment in Kansas City. Booked under the alias Richard Fowler, McDuff was arrested on 10 April 1992 as part of a Kansas City Police Department prostitution sting operation. Meanwhile federal officials were searching McDuff's Texas home, investigating the corporation of which he was vice-president and filing additional gun-possession charges against him. It was also at this time that the bodies of the women he had killed began to turn up. Alva Hank Worley confessed to his involvement with McDuff and their crimes on 20 April 1992, after previously having been reluctant to talk because of his fear of what McDuff would do to him if he ever found out.

A media blitz to locate McDuff was launched in Texas in late April, and within two weeks the US Marshals' Office received more than five hundred phone calls reporting sightings of the fugitive. Most were a waste of time. During this period, McDuff continued to believe that he was as close to being God as any human being could get. He did not seem to worry very much about the possibility that he might be wanted in connection with Melissa Northrup's abduction, even though he must have known that he had been seen by some passers-by and had left his vehicle in the parking lot of the Quik Pak where Northrup worked. He carried on with his life, doing and dealing drugs, drinking heavily, and having rough sex with prostitutes. By changing his name to Richard Fowler, it seemed to McDuff that all he had to do to remain a free man was to carry on his existence under an assumed name. He had reached the pinnacle of the evolutionary model of serial murder. The only thing that awaited him was the fall back into reality, something he had not been acquainted with for several decades.

The search for the fugitive intensified in the spring of 1992, and the case of Melissa Northrup's abduction appeared on an episode of the television show *America's Most Wanted*. Two days after the show aired, one of McDuff's co-workers, who knew the serial killer as Richard Fowler, phoned in to report that Fowler resembled the wanted man. Fingerprints of both Fowler and McDuff were compared and police quickly realised that they had found their man. McDuff was arrested on 4 May 1992. Two days later, he was charged in a federal court with distribution of LSD and felony possession of a firearm. McDuff continued to play the role that he had been taught as a child. He figured that if he pretended to be innocent and denied any involvement or connection with the charges, he would be let go. He had evolved to the point where he no longer believed that anyone would ever doubt his word, and that all he had to do was continually lie about his whereabouts and deny the charges. In this way, he would be released.

Finding himself behind bars once again did not have an adverse effect on McDuff, who continued to delude himself into believing that he was invincible. Rules did not apply to him, because he had elevated his consciousness to a higher state of being, which made him necessarily better than everyone else and accountable only to himself. In September 1992, McDuff switched cells with another inmate because he wanted to have sexual intercourse with a different cellmate. After several hours of rough sex, McDuff's sexual partner ratted him out to authorities, and McDuff was placed in isolation.

During his trial for the murder of Melissa Northrup, McDuff so angered his court-appointed attorneys that they requested to be removed from the case, since their client was not allowing them to provide him with an adequate defence. The motion was denied, and McDuff continued to sabotage his defence by testifying on his own behalf. The serial killer, completely overtaken by his evolution into a self-created God, believed that all he had to do in order to convince the jury of his innocence was to claim he had nothing to do with the murder. For an hour and a half, McDuff repeatedly denied any knowledge of the disappearance and murder of Melissa Northrup, despite the evidence that pointed to him as the murderer. Confidently, McDuff laughed at the prosecution's questions and smiled and waved at his mother and other members of his family while he was being questioned. The tactic failed, and in the end McDuff was convicted of the murder and sentenced to death for a second time. McDuff would also be convicted and sentenced to death for the murder of Colleen Reed.

As a result of the Kenneth Allen McDuff fiasco, several McDuff Laws were passed, which stated that if a defendant received a life sentence after 1 September 1993 for the commission of the crime of capital murder, he must serve at least forty years before being eligible for parole. When the defendant became eligible for parole, in order to be released he would have to receive a two-thirds vote in favour of parole from the eighteen-member Board of Pardons and Paroles.

Before Kenneth McDuff was executed by the state of Texas on 17 November 1998, he confessed to the murders of Regenia Moore, Brenda Thompson and Valencia Kay Joshua through a series of confidential informants employed by the state of Texas. Their remains were recovered, but McDuff never faced charges in any of these murders.

As an example of the evolutionary model of serial murder, Kenneth McDuff meets and exceeds the standards by which the model was created. He had completely and psychotically distanced himself from all other human beings, believing totally, until the day he was executed, that they existed for the sole purpose of satisfying his own perverse needs. Totally self absorbed, McDuff joked frequently that he could only commit three murders a day because it was too tiring for him to dig more than that number of graves in one 24-hour period. He did not recognise any human emotions, and nor did he experience or exhibit them himself. He felt no remorse, not even for the situations he found himself in, although such remorse has characteristically been experienced and outwardly projected by serial killers who fit into the other models presented in this book. There was moreover no recognition on his part that he had ever done anything wrong. The reasons for his crimes and for being placed on death row twice had to do with other people and their incompetence. In his mind and through his words, McDuff painted the picture that he was an innocent person who had been misunderstood, mistreated and deceived.

His world view, coupled with his drug addiction and his total disregard for human life, were all contributory components into his evolution as a serial killer. In his case, McDuff also had other outside influences that created the monster inside him, a monster that broke free to wreak unbridled havoc across the state of Texas. These influences included the reinforcing and permissive attitude his mother took towards his misbehaviour as a youth, the failure of the criminal justice system to prevent McDuff from leaving prison on at least two occasions, and the willingness and complacency demonstrated by both Roy Dale Green and Alva Hank Worley, who allowed McDuff to commit heinous acts of violence in front of their eyes without attempting to stop him until the deed had been done. The fear which McDuff struck in others and the knowledge that he could make people afraid of him would allow him to do whatever he wanted, and had a profound effect on McDuff's evolution from petty criminal to convicted serial murderer. In the end, just as in the case of Randy Kraft, it was McDuff's own false conceptions of power and status that eventually led to his downfall. As with all serial killers who fit the evolutionary profile, McDuff was so concerned with being above everyone else that he failed to realise that not everyone subscribed to his particular theory of reality.

CONCLUSION

Serial killers inhabit a frightening place in our collective consciousness. The average American has only a one in 13,000 chance of being murdered. The chance of becoming a victim of multiple murder is even less likely; fewer than 4% of murder victims fall into this category. The atrocious nature of this brutal crime, however, ensures that it will continue to dominate headlines and airwaves for the foreseeable future. In many ways, it is the most challenging crime to understand. It is for this reason that a great many resources are marshalled to deal with it, yet despite a collaborative effort, the majority of homicides remain unsolved.

The theories examined in this book often overlap one another, perhaps because they follow a central theme. Regardless of the approach favoured by the reader, each theory suggests that serial killers suffer from a pervasive pattern of low self-esteem. Some killers recognise this pattern as a self-defeating cycle, while others insist that the problem belongs to everyone else. The distinction between *overt* and *covert* manifestations is nothing more than a generalisation, designed to help researchers and investigators determine a frame of reference for predicting behaviour. It borrows from the disciplines of psychology, sociology and physiology. By themselves, each field has contributed an overwhelming amount of information on the subject of episodic homicidal behaviour, and factored together, these contributions increase our resources exponentially. And yet still more is needed.

No single school of thought can claim ultimate authority on the subject. Forensic science has provided some of the best tools for identifying and convicting offenders, but it cannot predict the determining causes of serial murder. Likewise, psychological profiling can provide a map of probable symptoms, but generally falls short of uncovering an offender's motivations. Many people are involved in building a house. It would be unthinkable not to include an architect, a surveyor, a contractor and a construction crew. Each person has an important role to play, interdependent with each other. Imagine all the things that could go wrong if the contractor did not communicate with the surveyor, or failed to examine the architect's blueprint. As in the construction of a house, investigators of serial homicide must communicate with experts from a variety of fields and utilise all available resources.

The most important question regarding serial homicide is whether or not it can be prevented. Not only is prevention possible – it is known to have occurred. The prison system is the most obvious evidence of this. But how can one measure true prevention, the type that precedes the commission of the crime? It is easy to suggest that such a question has no answer. But to those who have made it their chosen profession to respond to the afflictions of others, the answer is that it *can* be done. We will probably never know just how many would-be serial killers have been diverted from the homicidal path. What is certain, however, is that this divergence, when it occurs, takes place as a result of an appropriate level of early intervention. Unfortunately, this does not happen until someone is able to recognise a need. The failure to mitigate the problem of serial murder is a failure of the system to integrate its many available resources.

Agencies must not be territorial. A spirit of co-operation is necessary to bring an end to humankind's most perplexing problem. After all, it is our failure to recognise the needs of others, and to act on them, that has produced a fertile environment for murder. The motivations that drive a person to commit murder are cultivated in the darkest places of the mind, but they do not grow without prolonged exposure to abuse and abandonment. Rejection, in its various forms, has turned people against one another. This circumstance is the darkest truth of all.

BIBLIOGRAPHY

American Psychiatric Association (1994) *Diagnostic and Statistical Manual of Mental Disorders* (4th ed.). Washington, DC.

Armour, N. (1995, 10 November) 'Suspected serial killer driven by "murdering spirit," minister says.' Associated Press.

Davis, D. (1991) *The Milwaukee Murders*, St Martin's Press, New York.

Emerick, R. L., Gray, S. R., & Gray, S. L. (2001, September) *Sexual Behavior Program: Alternatives to Sexual Misbehavior*, Unpublished manual.

Englade, K. (1989) *Cellar of Horror*, St Martin's Press, New York.

Farr, L. (1992) *The Sunset Murders*, Pocket Books, New York.

Federal Bureau of Investigation (1988) *FBI Law Enforcement Bulletin*.

Hall, C., & Lindzey, G. (1970) *Theories of Personality*, John Wiley and Sons, New York.

Havill, A. (2001) *Born Evil*, St Martin's Press, New York.

Holmes, R., & DeBurger, J. (1988) *Serial Murder*, Sage Publications, Newbury Park, CA.

Keyes, E. (1976) *The Michigan Murders*, Pocket Books, New York.

King, G. (2003) *Keith Hunter Jesperson: the Happy Face Killer*, Courtroom Television Network LLC.

Kurtz, C. (2002) *Demons and Madmen*, Word Wrangler Publishing, Inc, Livingston, MT.

Lane, B., & Gregg, W. (1992) *The Encyclopedia of Serial Killers*. Berkley Books, New York.

McDougal, D. (1992) *Angel of Darkness*, Warner Books, Inc, New York.

Norris, J. (1992) *Arthur Shawcross: the Genesee River Killer*, Shadow Lawn Press, New York.

Ramsland, K. (2003) *John Norman Collins: the Co-Ed Killer*, Courtroom Television Network LLC.

Ramsland, K. (2003) *Richard Trenton Chase*, Courtroom Television Network LLC.

Rule, A. (1988) *Lust Killer*, Signet Books, New York.

Rule, A. (2001) *The Stranger Beside Me*, Signet Books, New York.

Steel, F. (2003) *Savage Weekend: Daniel Rolling*, Courtroom Television Network LLC.

Wilson, C. (2000) *The History of Murder*, Carroll and Graf Publishers, Inc, New York.